365 Inspirations

One Minute Insights for Love Success and Happiness

by Mark Rose

Claflin Media Group

Acknowledgments

My heartfelt thanks go out to everyone who helped and supported me throughout this process, especially my wife, Donna, and my daughter, Jo Beth, two amazing and beautiful people who constantly give me encouragement and love. Thanks also to my editor, Anne Rose, who transforms my thoughts and words into a cohesive message.

And a special thanks to all my generous friends and fans who supported my Kickstarter campaign. Without you this book would not have gotten published. By sharing my vision, you have helped to make my dream a reality. Much love to all of you.

And last, but certainly not least, a huge THANK YOU, THANK YOU, THANK YOU to the big supporters of my Kickstarter campaign.

Rebecca Richardson
Georgina Thompson
Bill Sutton

I am awed by your generosity, your kindness, and your faith in me. May your lives always be filled with love, laughter, and all of God's blessings.

www.365inspirations.net

Thanks again. If you enjoy this book, please look at my
other offerings and check out my websites,
www.AcceptHappinessNow.com
and
www.HeavenOnEarthProject.com.
You can also e-mail me from either site. I will be happy to
answer any questions you have.
You can also visit my blog at
www.NormalSucks.net

Introduction

Thank you for purchasing this book and trying to make yourself more successful. The key to a more prosperous world is each of us making ourselves more successful.

This book is a little different than most. There are no chapters, and I don't expect you to read it straight through. There are 366 quotes from some of the most intelligent, clever, learned, and spiritual teachers throughout history. After each quote are my thoughts on its meaning and how to apply its wisdom to your life.

Read the daily message each morning and work on applying that message to your life that day. Continue doing this throughout the year to reinforce the flow of positive energy into your life and accustom yourself to beginning each day with inspired, uplifting ideas that can truly transform your thinking. There will be some messages you will identify with more than others. If there is one you don't agree with or that doesn't resonate with you, simply think about it or move on. Certain themes repeat throughout the book. The repetition of these themes allows you to view them from different perspectives and ponder them in order to assimilate their truth and wisdom.

My hope is that after applying these basic principals to your life, you will be more loving, happier, and more successful. When you notice changes in the way you think or the way you view life, share these ideas with the people around you, for spreading love and happiness is indeed our highest purpose.

January 1

"We will open the book. Its pages are blank. We are going to put words on them ourselves. The book is called Opportunity and its first chapter is New Year's Day."
~ Edith Lovejoy Pierce

Make today the beginning of your new life. What will you do? What changes will you make? If you want to keep getting what you've been getting, then keep doing what you've been doing. But if you want the rest of your life to be different, you must do things differently. Scary? Yes. Impossible? No.

Today think about where you want to be in your new life and then plan what you have to do to get there.

January 2

"Trying to change the outer is like seeing your unclean or unshaven face in the mirror and trying to shave or clean the mirror."~ Joe Vitale

The world you live in is a reflection of you. For the outside world to change, you must first change yourself. You attract what you are. If you are generous, your world will be generous. If you are abundant, your world will be abundant. If you are upset , your world will be upsetting. You have the power to change yourself on the inside. Then and only then will your outer world change.

Hold the feelings of what you want in your world. Do you desire to live in a peaceful, loving world? Then feel peace and love. Do you wish to live in a prosperous world? Then feel prosperous. Be what you want to see.

Today remember the world you see is just a reflection of you.

January 3

"When you change your attitude towards another, he must change his attitude towards you."~ Neville Goddard

From time to time we meet a person with whom we don't get along. Sometimes we are forced to be around this person. He could be a relative or a coworker. When we experience his not liking us, we usually react by not liking him. Then he reacts with more negativity, and a cycle begins. To change the cycle, treat him with kindness. In time he will start to treat you with kindness. It is inevitable.

Today choose someone with whom you have not gotten along and be nice to him. If he is not nice in return, keep being nice. His attitude will change.

January 4

"Forgiveness means letting go of the past."
~ Gerald Jampolsky

We all have a story, and most of the stories involve what someone did to us. Now is the time to let go of all those past hurts and resentments. Forgive that person and let go of your story. When you forgive someone, you do not need to tell him, although if you can that would be great.

Forgiveness is a gift you give yourself. If you are angry with someone you haven't spoken to in years, do you think he cares? He may have forgotten your name and who you are.

You need to forgive him so you can release the pain and anger you feel.

Forgive so you can be free. You can't change the events of the past, but if you continue to live in the past, your future will continue to be tainted by it.

Today forgive someone and let go of the past.

January 5

"Accept responsibility for your life. Know that it is you who will get you where you want to go, no one else."~ Les Brown

When you accept responsibility for where you are, you then have the power to determine where you are going. When you blame someone or something else for your situation, you are stuck in that situation until the someone or something changes.

When you complain that you can't meet the love of your life because there are no single people in your town, you are giving away your power, and the only way for you to meet the right person is to move. However, when you say, I have not done all that I can to meet the right person, you have the opportunity to change your future.

Stop blaming other people and situations. There are people in similar situations to yours who have succeeded in creating the outcome you desire. The difference is in you, and you can make the biggest difference in your life.

Today take responsibility.

January 6

"When people talk, listen completely. Most people never listen."~ Ernest Hemingway

Everyone loves a great listener, and the easiest way to have people like and respect you is to listen to them. Listen with your heart. Don't just hear the words, hear the meaning behind the words. Often when people are speaking, we are busy thinking about what we are going to say. Stop doing that and focus on the person who is talking. He is letting you get to know him. He is opening up his soul to you. Listen to his words and how the words are spoken. Watch his body language and facial expressions, and feel the energy he is sending out.

Most people never listen because they are focused on themselves. Imagine that the person you are talking to is the most important person in the world, and he is telling you the most important and interesting thing you have ever heard.

Today listen like you have never listened before.

January 7

"By letting it go, it all gets done. The world is won by those who let it go. But when you try and try, the world is beyond the winning."~ Lao Tzu

Look at nature. Mother nature does not force things to happen, but rather lets things happen. Imagine life as a river. You can try to force the river to do something that it doesn't want to do, or you can allow it to flow. When you use force against the river, it just flows around you. Even the largest dams must let the water out, or eventually the water will overflow. Life is the same way. It must flow, and when you try to block the flow of life, life flows around you.

Stop trying to fight life and enjoy it. Flow with life. Move around in the flow and find the experiences you wish. Then allow the flow to carry you to the next experience. Stop resisting. When you let go, the things you do not want will just flow away.

Today let go and let God.

January 8

"Spiritual evolution occurs as the result of removing obstacles and not actually acquiring anything new."~ David R. Hawkins

As infants we are all very spiritually evolved. We are born pure, and we learn limitations and lack as we grow. We are taught to think like the people around us, and we often grow up to have similar beliefs. To continue to grow, we must examine these beliefs and cast aside the ones that no longer serve us. To grow we must find the spiritual beliefs that we agree with and release the thoughts that do not align with these spiritual beliefs.

Enlightenment is like the sun. The sun is always shining. We just may not be able to see it. Your enlightenment is in you. You just need to remove the blocks to let it out.

Today let go of a belief that is not serving you.

January 9

"Only you have the power to decide your mood. You can keep that power or give it away."~ Mark Rose

Life is determined not by the events in your life but how you react to those events. You have the choice to be happy, and no person or event can change your mood. The events of your day can only affect your mood if you choose to let them.

Know this. You are in control of your mind. Your thoughts determine your emotions, and you control your thoughts. The next time you notice yourself getting upset, think about something that makes you happy - your children, a vacation, your friends, or any other happy thought. When you change your thoughts, you will change your feelings.

Today remember that no one has the power to make you happy, sad, or mad. It is your choice. I choose happiness. Your choice is up to you.

January 10

"Whoever is happy will make others happy, too."
~ Mark Twain

Happiness is contagious. If you walk into a room with a few friends in it and you are not consciously choosing your mood, you will take on the mood of the people around you. If they are happy, you will be happy. If they are mad, you will become mad. This is the same principal as the "mob mentality."

However, if you are choosing to be happy, you can switch the mood of the people around you. You can create happiness just by being happy.

Today choose to be happy.

January 11

"You cannot exercise much power without gratitude because it is gratitude that keeps you connected with power."
~ Wallace Wattles

Science has proven that everything is energy, and the energy that people emit is the result of the emotions they are experiencing at any given time. Energy is like a boomerang. The energy you send out returns to you, and gratitude is powerful, positive energy. By being grateful for everything that shows up in your life, you are exercising the divine power within you to claim even more to be grateful for. Many people are not aware of the incredible power of gratitude.

And when you combine the energy of gratitude with the energy of love, there is nothing in this world that you can't do or have. The power of gratitude and the power of love are at your fingertips. They are gifts from God, and they are the most wonderful feelings you can experience. Without them your world will seem hostile and uncaring, but with them your life will be all you ever wanted it to be.

Allow gratitude and love to be the energies you give to the world. Feel gratitude and love for everything in your life, and you will tap into the power of the universe.

Today feel grateful, and combine it with love.

January 12

"All you need is love, love. Love is all you need."
~ John Lennon

I am sure you have heard this before. "All You Need is Love" was a number one hit for the Beatles and was recorded by other artists almost twenty times. The question, however, is not was it popular, but is it true?

I believe it is. I think Mother Theresa is proof. She spent her life giving love, and everything she needed was provided for her. Her life may not be what you want for your life, so how you give love may look different, but love is still the answer.

When I look at my life and the times I have done something out of pure love, the results were always amazing. When I try to force something, the results are not always what I had hoped for.

As you spread love to others, and they spread it to someone else, the world will eventually be so filled with love that war will be a thing of the past, and we will all live in peace and harmony.

Today remember that God loves you, I love you, and that your love can change the world.

January 13

"It is not for you to judge the journey of another's soul. It is for you to decide who YOU are, not who another has been or has failed to be."~ Neale Donald Walsch

Many people spend their time thinking about what other people are doing. More precisely they spend their time judging what other people are doing. When you are concentrating on how much better you are, you prevent yourself from doing two things.

First, you keep yourself from doing anything productive because judging others is not productive. And second, you keep yourself from accepting that person. The result of not doing anything productive is obvious. However, not accepting others is even more detrimental. When you cannot accept someone for who he is, you are set up for disappointment. Either your expectations will be too high or too low, and neither is good.

When you can eliminate those judgements, you are free to discover who you are. Looking at yourself can be hard, but it is the path to making yourself better, not better than another, but better than you used to be. Look at yourself and see how you can improve.

Today accept others for who they are and live your life getting better every day.

January 14

"Be at least as interested in what goes on inside you as what happens outside. If you get the inside right, the outside will fall into place."~ Eckhart Tolle

The events of your life do not determine your life. Your reaction to those events does. The child of a criminal can grow up to become a criminal and say, "It's in my genes. I never had a chance," or he can grow up to say, "I saw how my criminal parent lived, and I don't want that for my life." Similar situations with different results.

Stop caring so much about what happens to you and more about how to handle those situations so they can benefit you.

Today remember life is an inside job.

January 15

"To live a pure unselfish life, one must count nothing as one's own in the midst of abundance."~ Buddha

The Native Americans knew this. They lived on the land and were a part of nature. They never overused any resource, and they lived as a tribe, all helping one another. When the tribe did well, they all did well individually.

Now imagine that everything you have is on loan, not yours to keep, just yours to use for now. I am not trying to convince you to live without things in your life. I am talking about being in the world but not of the world. Your happiness is not in your stuff. It isn't in your friends and family. It isn't even in your spouse. Your happiness is in you.

When you let go of your attachment to stuff, it is easier to be happy. You stop worrying about what may happen to the stuff, and you start to enjoy life. You are not concerned about what other people have because you are not concerned about what you have. You are in the world and experiencing all of the joys and the pains of the world, and you are happy regardless of what happens.

Today be in the world but not of the world.

January 16

"When you find peace within yourself, you become the kind of person who can live at peace with others."~ Peace Pilgrim

It has been said that the world is a mirror, reflecting back who you are. If you are a peaceful person, you will live in a peaceful world. If you are an angry person, you will find yourself in an angry world. And the world doesn't care.

By finding the love inside you, the peace that you truly are, your world will transform. You will experience more peace and love in your everyday life. The people around you will respond to your energy. Your life will flow more smoothly.

Today allow the real you to come out. Discard your anger, fear, and worry.

January 17

"It's not the events of our lives that shape us, but our beliefs as to what those events mean."~ Tony Robbins

E+R=O   Event + Reaction = Outcome

Many people experience similar events yet have different reactions. After a hardship some people use the event as an excuse. Others use it as a reason.

" My spouse died when I was 35. Please feel sorry for me," is an excuse to stay stuck in the past and elicit pity. "My spouse died when I was 35. That made me realize how fragile life is, so I live every day to the fullest," is a reason to embrace life. Same event. Different reaction.

Think of the events in your life. Are you using those events to empower your life or hold you back? Do you have a story? Your story is likely holding you back. When you change the way you look at things, when you change your story, your world will change.

Today think about how you have reacted in the past. Did your reactions help you or hurt you, and can you change your beliefs about those events?

January 18

"Worrying about tomorrow is the best way to screw up today."~ Dennis Leary

Focus on this moment. The only time you can ever do anything is now. If there is something you can do to prevent a problem, do it. If there is a situation that is beyond your control, then let it happen. In either case, worrying just wastes your energy and the present moment.

The world can be divided into two categories - things you can control and things you can't control. The list of things you can control is short. It only contains you. That's it. The list of things you can't control contains everything else.

Focus on what you can control. Do all you can do right now and tomorrow will take care of itself.

Today stop worrying and focus on this moment.

January 19

"Men for the sake of getting a living, forget to live."
~ Margaret Fuller

People often get so caught up in the rat race that they forget to live. Life is meant to be fun, not work. We are here to enjoy ourselves. We are here to experience all of the wonderful gifts that the world has to give us.

Go to work and support your family, but give up the need for more and simply enjoy what you have now. You don't know what tomorrow will bring. If you spend all of your time preparing for a better tomorrow, you may not live to enjoy it. Today live in the moment and enjoy where you are.

January 20

"If you want others to be happy, practice compassion. If you want to be happy, practice compassion."~ Dalai Lama

In other words, the easiest way to find happiness is to be compassionate. By practicing compassion, you empathize with other people. Try to see things from their point of view and be nice.

Sounds like advice you would get from your grandmother doesn't it? I have found that most of the secrets to a happy, fulfilled life are not secrets at all. They are the common sense advice you have heard your whole life. The only secret is how to apply them.

When you interact with other people, be there. Focus on the person you are with. Pay attention to what he says, how he says it, and his body language. When you are focused on him, it will be much easier to be compassionate.

Today practice compassion.

January 21

"If the only prayer you ever say in your entire life is thank you, it will be enough."~ Meister Eckhart

Many people's prayers look like letters to Santa Claus. Stop praying for what you don't have and be thankful for what you do have. This simple shift in thinking can transform your life. When you appreciate what you have, you are opening yourself up for more to be thankful for.

Gratitude is a gift you give yourself. When you are grateful, the world is more loving.

Today and every day start your morning with a prayer of gratitude and see how many more things there are to be thankful for.

January 22

"And as we let our own light shine, we unconsciously give other people permission to do the same."
~ Marianne Williamson

Have you ever had great news to tell someone, but before you could get it out she told you about some horrible event that just happened to her? Did you share your good news or did you avoid showing that you where happy while she was sad?

We often try to match the mood of the people around us. Sometimes this is conscious, but most of the time it happens without our realizing it. But when you know you have this ability, you can use it to brighten any room you walk into. When you are happy and loving, that energy can spread to others. Your positive attitude actually gives others permission to be loving too.

Today brighten every room you walk into.

January 23
"If you want to be happy, be happy."~ Leo Tolstoy

The only thing between you and your happiness is you. I know there are times when you would like to blame someone or something because you are unhappy, but placing the blame outside of yourself is an exercise in futility. If you are happy, it is because you choose to be, and if you are unhappy, it is because you choose to be. You may not realize that you are making that choice, but you are.

When you realize that you can choose to be happy, happiness is easily found. You just need to know that you can make that choice. Try it now. Choose to be happy. You may need to think of a happy event or a person you care about, but you can do it. The more you practice, the easier it will be, and soon you will be able to choose to be happy at any time.

Today choose to be happy.

January 24
"Any man worth his salt will stick up for what he believes right, but it takes a slightly better man to acknowledge instantly and without reservation that he is in error."
~ Andrew Jackson

There are people who never admit they are wrong. There are also people who readily change their beliefs to be accepted by others. These conditions are commonly referred to as arrogance or a lack of self esteem. Both can lead to problems.

Everyone makes mistakes, but not everyone has the strength or character to admit when he is wrong. Learning from your mistakes and freely admitting them is what takes someone from good to great.

Stand up for what you believe is right, but by all means, if you discover you are in error, admit it.

Today look at your life. Is there a decision you made that was wrong? If so, admit you made a mistake and move on.

January 25

"What is the opposite of abundance? It's not scarcity. It's greed. Greed is the belief that there is not enough for everyone, so you'd better grab yours now. What is the opposite of love? It's not hate. It's fear. Fear is the belief that someone or something can hurt you."~ Robert G. Allen

What do you believe? Do you believe there is enough for everyone, or do you believe in lack? If you can remove the idea of lack from your thoughts, then lack will be removed from your life.

Do you believe you are vulnerable? Do you believe you can be hurt? When you remove the idea of injury from your thoughts, you remove the idea of injury from your life.

Lack and injury are ideas we have created for ourselves. The universe is limitless, so what we desire is available for us now. We are spirits having a human experience. Your spirit cannot be hurt or destroyed, so the real you cannot be hurt.

Today look at your beliefs and know that you are eternal and abundant.

January 26

"Conflict cannot survive without your participation."
~ Wayne Dyer

Any conflict or argument takes two people with different viewpoints. The easiest way to end any conflict is to get rid of the idea that you are right and the other person is wrong. Be willing to listen to an opposing viewpoint, even if you don't agree with it. Then say something like, "I never looked at it that way," or "Thank you for sharing your point of view," or even, "I will have to look into this further, but thanks for sharing what you know."

It comes down to the question, do you want to be happy, or do you want to be right? I would much rather be happy. Realistically, if you're having an argument with someone, you're probably not going to change his mind, and he's not going to change yours. So why get involved in the discussion in the first place? Just decide to be happy, and don't take part in petty little arguments.

This is a great philosophy to live by. Allow people to believe what they want to believe and be who they choose to be. Let go of the need to have everyone agree with your point of view. It will never happen anyway. Live your life content in your own beliefs. Having your peace of mind is more important than giving someone a piece of your mind. Let go of petty little conflicts and just be happy.

Today decide to avoid conflict.

January 27

"Be careful the environment you choose for it will shape you; be careful the friends you choose for you will become like them."~ W. Clement Stone

We have all seen this. When two people who don't see each other very often get together, they act differently because they fall back into their old patterns. But this can also be true of the people you spend the most time with. People who spend a lot of time together often act like each other. This can be good.

If a person joins a group because he aspires to be like the people in the group, then being around them will likely cause changes in him. The influence of the group is usually stronger than the influence of one person. But if that person who wants to grow and change spends time with a group of people who are not moving in the direction he wants to go, his progress can be hampered.

And the same is also true of your environment. Are you surrounded by things that are helping you or hurting you? If you want to be peaceful and loving, avoid images, TV shows, and movies that depict violence. If you want to be wealthy, fill your environment with signs of wealth.

Today examine your friends and your environment and start to move in the direction you want to go.

January 28

"If you are confident in your beliefs then why are you getting upset?"~ Ben Schoeffler

Have you ever been accused of being something that you know you are not? Did it bother you? If someone told you they didn't like your pink hair, even though your hair is clearly not pink, would it bother you? Of course not. You would just think the person was nuts or color blind, and you'd move on. What if someone accused you of being racist, or narrow minded, or petty, or jealous, or some other trait you certainly don't believe you are. Would that bother you? If so, it may be that you are not so sure of your convictions.

When you believe something with all of your being, you won't get upset if someone disagrees with those beliefs or challenges them. When you doubt your beliefs, an accusation against those beliefs may upset you and cause you to want to defend them. When you defend your beliefs, are you trying to convince the other person or yourself?

Look at what upsets you. Examine why you are upset and see if you are upset for the reason you think. It may just be that someone sees something in you that you see too.

Today be confident in your beliefs and let others believe what they want.

January 29

"Be who you are and say what you feel because those who mind don't matter and those who matter don't mind."
~ Dr. Seuss

I would rather be hated for who I am than loved for who I am not. When you try to become someone you are not, it's like building a cage that you have to live in. The more you pretend to be someone you are not, the more you have to pretend. Give up your pretending and be yourself.

When you are yourself, the people who care about you will be happy for you. And the people who want you to be something you are not are not the people you need in your life.

Today be yourself.

January 30

"Have the courage to act instead of react."
~ Darlene Larson Jenks

Reacting is easy. An event happens and we do what we feel like doing. Reacting also gives us a built in excuse. "I just reacted," or "I didn't have time to plan," or "I don't know what came over me." All of these excuses come from reacting, and that allows us as well as others to hold us to a lower standard.

The way to accomplish something is to act. Have a plan and execute that plan regardless of what happens.

Think about building a house. There are lots of little issues that can come up. The weather is bad. One of the workers is sick. We are out of material. The subcontractor isn't on schedule. Countless little issues could derail the project, but the contractor has a set of blueprints, a plan, and as long as everyone sticks to the plan, the house will be built.

Today plan your day in advance, know what you want to get done, have a list, and you will be able to get more accomplished.

January 31

"Rules help fools reach mediocrity. Beyond that, they have no function."~ Fred Hinegardner

Think about all of the great accomplishments in history. The people who made those accomplishments all broke rules. There used to be a rule that said humans can't fly. The Wright Brothers broke that rule.

Until May 6th 1954, the rule said that no human could run a mile in less than four minutes. Roger Banister broke that rule, and within months several other men also ran a mile in less than four minutes.

Great works of art are studied to determine what rules others should follow to create their own great works of art. But artists who create truly great works of art are the ones who don't follow the rules. They are the ones who break them. They are the ones who make their own rules.

Look at your life and your work. Are there rules that govern your life that are keeping you from greatness? Can you break those rules? Try something different. If it works, great. If it doesn't, then try something else. You can do more than the rules will allow.

Today make your own rules.

February 1

"The world around you will not transform unless you transform yourself."~ Cesar Milan

I am a big fan of Cesar (The Dog Whisperer). His recurring theme is that if you want your dog to behave better, you need to give your dog good energy. In other words, if you are stressed or anxious, your dog will be stressed and anxious. Dogs don't care about clothes, cars, status, or money. All they understand is energy. Dogs are very in tune to energy, and when people change their energy and take control, they get control of their dog and also of their lives.

You can change anything in your life by changing your energy. People often talk about how much "luck" they have. There's no such thing as luck. It's energy, and most people's energy stays the same. You can change your energy and transform yourself by changing your attitude. Then your world will transform.

Today think about how you are feeling and what energy you are putting into the world.

February 2

"Never walk away from failure. On the contrary, study it carefully and imaginatively for its hidden assets."
~ Michael Korda

If you have never failed, you have never taken a risk. If you have never taken a risk, you are not growing. To grow we must expand our limits by doing things that seem risky.

When things don't go the way we hoped they would, the secret is to learn from the experience. But we need to learn the right lesson. If you burn your hand on the stove, you could learn never to touch the stove again, or you could learn to check if the stove is on first. One lesson limits us. The other lesson helps us.

Look at the failures in your life and the lessons you have learned. Are you taking enough risk to continue growing? Have the lessons you have learned helped you or limited you? Can you reevaluate the event and change the lesson?

Today learn from your mistakes, but make sure you learn the right lesson.

February 3

"Happiness is our natural state. Happiness is the natural state of little children, to whom the kingdom belongs until they have been polluted and contaminated by the stupidity of society and culture."~ Anthony deMello

Society doesn't teach children to be unhappy, but it does teach them that other things are more important than happiness. We teach our children to strive for good grades and to be good athletes, musicians, or even artists. We teach our children to fit in and follow the rules. We make lots of things more important than happiness. The big irony is that we want them to do all of these things so they can be happy.

People often do not know what it takes to be happy. If you ask people what it takes to be happy, most would say lots of money, or lots of friends, or even prestige and status. This is what society teaches, and so we take perfectly normal, happy children and tell them they need these things to be happy. But the truth is, most children are already happy. Perhaps if adults tried to be more like children instead of trying to make children more like adults, they'd be happier.

Know that your natural state is happiness. You just need to lose the baggage that society has given you so that you can experience that happiness.

Today choose to be happy.

February 4

"What separates the winners from the losers is how a person reacts to each new twist of fate."~ Donald Trump

Whatever your circumstances are, there are people in similar circumstances who have done better and others who have done worse than you are doing now. Stop focusing on the circumstances. What matters is how you react to them.

Your situation does not determine your life. Your actions do. Learn to stop reacting and take positive action.

Today act in your own best interest regardless of the circumstances facing you.

February 5

"A change in feeling is a change of destiny."
~ Neville Goddard

You control your destiny, not anyone else, just you. You get to choose how you react to the events in your life. You can view any event with a positive attitude and look for the best, or you can have a negative attitude and expect the worst.

When you have a positive attitude, you feel good. When you feel good, you see the good in situations. When you feel bad, you miss the good. The good is still there, but you are just not open to see it. By changing the way you feel from bad to good, you see the good more often.

The next time you feel bad, notice your feeling and change your mind. Decide to feel good. Just tell yourself you feel good. Then think about things you love, and you will start to feel good. Then you can continue your day feeling good.

Today feel good.

February 6

"I'd rather attempt to do something great and fail than attempt to do nothing and succeed."~ Robert H. Schuller

Whoever told you that failing was a horrible event was wrong, or at least they could be wrong. Failure is like every other event in your life. It has no meaning except the meaning you give it. If you attempt to accomplish a goal and you do not succeed, learn from your mistake and keep trying. Everyone who has ever done something great has also failed. Great things are great because they are not easy.

Dare something worthy. Dare to do something that will push you to the limits. Do something great, and if you do not succeed on the first attempt, keep trying. What is it that moves your spirit? What is it that you have a burning desire to do? Not something that you want the world to do, but that one great thing that is inside you trying to get out.

Today take one step to release your greatness.

February 7

"Be thankful for what you have; you'll end up having more. If you concentrate on what you don't have, you will never, ever have enough."~ Oprah Winfrey

It all comes down to focus. What you are focusing on is what you are giving your attention to. When you focus on lack, your subconscious mind keeps a look out for lack and does everything it can to make sure that lack shows up in your life. When you focus on your blessings, you are inviting more blessings, and your subconscious will look for more blessings for you.

Sometimes this can be difficult. When you have more bills than money, or when you are lonely and looking for that special person, it can be hard to focus on the good. One easy way to switch from fear to gratitude is with love. Think of the situation and say, "I love you." Tell the situation, the person, or even your bills, "I love you." Do this ten times and see if you don't feel better. And if you really want to feel good, say it one hundred times.

Today experience a miracle. Use love to change from fear to gratitude.

February 8

"The most important thing is to enjoy your life - to be happy. It's all that matters."~ Audrey Hepburn

Often people go through life working toward goals they think will bring them happiness. They spend time at a job they don't like or make sacrifices they wish they didn't have to make. They do this so they can achieve some arbitrary prize that they think will be the key to happiness. This doesn't work. Your ego is driving you toward these desires, and as soon as you reach them, your ego will point you toward some other goal. And the happiness you seek will only be yours for short moments.

Stop chasing your tail. Happiness is here right now, and when you let go of the thought that you need something outside of yourself to be happy, you will find that happiness is here for you. Decide to be happy and enjoy your life. Sure it is great to make a difference and help others, but make sure you enjoy your life too. You get to decide your mood, and nothing or no one can decide for you. Decide to be happy no matter what happens. Decide to enjoy life - all of its ups and downs and twists and turns.

Today decide to be happy and enjoy your life.

February 9

"When you fully realize that thought causes all, you will know there are never any limits that you yourself do not impose."
~ U.S. Andersen

What limits are you imposing on yourself?

Have you ever said,
" I am not smart enough."
" I don't have enough money."
" No one will ever want to go out with me."
" I won't get the promotion."
" I am not good enough."
These are all limiting statements.

Instead say,
"I am very smart."
"I always have enough money to do what I want and need to do."
"I am attractive and desirable."
"I know I'm going to get the promotion."
"I am great. I am a divine child of God, and God will help me through any difficulty."

When you tell yourself you can, then you will. When you ask yourself how, you will find a way. Difficulties and obstacles are the universe's way of asking you if you really want to fulfill your desires. Say yes to the universe and your problems will melt away. Stop limiting your greatness and open your life up to a world of possibilities.

Today stop imposing limitations on yourself.

February 10

"The measure of love is love without measure."
~ Saint Bernard of Clairvaux

Love with limitations is not love. Love with conditions is not love. Most people cannot grasp the true nature of God's love because we live in a world of conditional love. When people say they love each other, there is the possibility that in the future their love may be gone.

A man says he loves his wife, but if she has an affair and takes his money and his children, his love for her disappears.

God's love is different. God loves everyone no matter what he does or says. Religions have told us that there are things we must do to earn God's love. Please don't believe that. You can have no secrets from God, and God loves you exactly as you are. God's love cannot be measured because God loves everything completely.

You can learn to love completely. Start with a child, your child if you have one. Let him know you love him no matter what. Tell him you will love him if he gets straight A's or has to repeat a grade. Tell him your love won't waver whether he grows up to be a doctor or a ditch digger. And tell him that your love for him is not based on his love for you. You will love him the same if he gives you a hug and a kiss or if he never speaks to you. That kind of love allows a person to be himself, and there is no greater gift.

Today love unconditionally.

February 11

Forgive all who have offended you, not for them, but for yourself."~ Harriet Nelson

Let it go. Get over it. Move on with your life. Has anyone ever told you this? Now is the time to do it.

The past is gone. You can hold on to the pain of the past and allow it to destroy the happiness you could have today, or you can let go and live for today. When you live for today, you allow yourself to be happy.

When you forgive, you release the negative energy from you, not from the other person. The person who benefits is you. So get over it.

Today forgive one person.

February 12

"You have heard it said you shall love your neighbor and hate your enemy, but I say to you, love your enemies and pray for those who persecute you."~ Jesus Christ

It is easy to love those who love you. Being nice to your friends is not hard to do. Being nice to people you don't know takes a little more concentration, but it is fairly easy as well. The difficult part is loving those who persecute you and being nice to people you don't like and who don't like you.

Suggesting that you love everyone without giving you any insight or tools as to how to do that would not be helpful. You know that being nice to people is the best way to be, but how do you go about being nice to people who are mean, angry, and grumpy?

Fake it till you make it. I know it sounds silly, but give it a try. When you come across someone who is hard to be nice to, just tell him, "I love you." You don't need to say it out loud. In fact just saying it in your mind may be better. You don't even have to mean it. Just say, "I love you," over and over again. Before you talk to him, picture him in your mind, send him loving thoughts, and wish him the best. Keep doing this until you do mean it, and see if his attitude toward you changes.

By giving love to everyone, you are doing your part to make the world a better place. If everyone gave love instead of anger, hatred, or fear, the world would be more loving. Don't you want to live in a more loving place?

Today do your part. Give love.

February 13

"We come to love not by finding a perfect person, but by learning to see an imperfect person perfectly."~ Sam Keen

In the eyes of God we are all perfect. However, we judge one another to be less than perfect. When you start to see people as God sees them, you can love them as God loves them. When you start to love people as God loves them, you will experience the love that was strong enough to create the universe.

God views you as perfect. When we can start to see the perfection in others, we can begin to see the love in others as well and realize the love in us. Look for the love. It is there, and when you find it, your life will become less stressful and more peaceful.

Today love without judgement.

February 14

"When men and women are able to respect and accept their differences, then love has a chance to blossom."~ John Gray

We are all different. We have all experienced different things. When we can accept those differences without judgement, we are on our way to love. True love is acceptance. When you can accept people just the way they are, then you can love them. If you say, " I will love you if you act a certain way," that's not love. And this is true with all relationships, not just romantic ones. When you really love your kids, you accept them. And loving your boss, your coworkers, and even your friends is great too.

Today accept and love someone.

February 15

"You can make more friends in two months by becoming interested in other people than you can in two years by trying to get people interested in you."~ Dale Carnegie

Making connections is one of the keys to success. If you have a job, you have a boss and co-workers. If you own a business, you have employees and customers. There are vendors, competitors, and other businesses to deal with too. Outside of work you have family, neighbors, and friends. All of these people are more concerned with their own lives than they are with yours.

When you focus on what is important to the people you are with, they will view you in a positive light. You will become someone they like and want to spend time with. Eventually you can share what is important to you, but first take a real interest in them, and listen to what they have to say. You may have to listen for an hour, a week, or a month, but it will be time well spent because you will be laying the groundwork for a friendship that could last a lifetime.

Today become a friend by listening.

February 16
"Events have no meaning except the meaning you give them."
~ Unknown

Keep this in mind and look at everything as a blessing. Rejoice that your car broke down. Celebrate that you got fired from your job. Be happy to receive bills in the mail.

When you look at every event as a blessing, then your life will be filled with blessings. Maybe your car breaking down prevented you from being in an accident. Maybe it forced you to take a much needed day off work. Or maybe it was just an opportunity to share your abundance with someone who needed it.

I can't explain the reason for every occurrence in your life, but I do know they are all blessings. And when you see that, your life will be transformed.

Today count your blessings. Every breath, every moment is a new blessing just waiting to be realized.

February 17

"Opportunities are usually disguised as hard work, so most people don't recognize them."~ Ann Landers

Many times when people complete a great accomplishment, they say it was easy because all the pieces just fell into place to make finishing the job possible. But they also recognized the opportunity, and regardless of the hard work that was required, they took on the endeavor.

Problems, hard work, and opportunities are all good friends, and they often show up together. Don't be afraid of hard work. Train yourself to find the opportunity instead of focusing on the problem.

Today find the opportunity in what you are doing. Opportunities are all around us. We just need to recognize them.

February 18

"Fear defeats more people than any other one thing in the world."~ Ralph Waldo Emerson

Fear immobilizes you. When you are afraid that you may not get the results you desire, you end up doing nothing at all. When you do nothing, you eliminate the possibility of success.

However, when you take action, you may or may not get the results you want, but at least you took action. If you don't take any action, you won't get any results.

Today allow yourself to be free of fear and take inspired action.

February 19

"If it is peace you want, seek to change yourself, not other people. It is easier to protect your feet with slippers than to carpet the whole of the earth."~ Anthony deMello

Are you tying to carpet the world? Do you look at the world and see anything other than perfection? I know it is hard to see the perfection of the world and of other people, but believe me, everyone is perfect and the world is in perfect harmony.

If you cannot see that, then the thing that needs to be changed is you. If your picnic is ruined by the rain, is the problem with you or with the rain? When someone breaks a law or does something mean, is the problem with the person or with how you feel about their actions? My guess is that seeing the rain as perfect is easier than seeing the person as perfect, but both are true.

Give up your idea that the world needs to change. Change yourself to see the world as perfect. Then you will be happy.

Today examine how you see the world and decide if it is time for a change.

February 20

"Imagine all the people living life in peace. You may say I'm a dreamer, but I'm not the only one. I hope someday you'll join us, and the world will be as one."~ John Lennon

Peace in the world begins with you. There are people who have chosen to live a life of peace. As that number grows, the world becomes a more peaceful place.

Choose to live a life of peace. Be the source of peace in your home, your workplace, and the world.

Today choose peace.

February 21

"One of the greatest gifts you can give to anyone is the gift of attention."~ Jim Rohn

When you talk to friends, family members, coworkers, customers, or anyone else, focus on them. Cherish the time you have with them and give them all of your attention. There is no better way to express to them that you care.

Often when we are talking to people, we are thinking about what we want to say, or we are thinking about something else altogether. When you catch yourself doing this, switch back to paying attention to the person you are with.

Wherever your body is, make sure your mind is there too. Focus on the people you come in contact with. Make the person you are with the most important person in the world. Give him your full and complete attention.

Today be present.

February 22
"It is a sin to be poor."~ Charles Fillmore

I have said that wealth is not the key to happiness, but neither is poverty.

You can attract wealth into your life with two steps. First, do what you love and love what you do, and second, change your thoughts about money.

Money is not good or evil. Money amplifies the effect a person has. Money in the hands of someone who wants to help the world will allow him to help more people.

The Divine Creator supplies everything in abundance. You only need to drop your negative feelings about money to experience abundance in your finances. Release your fear of lack and know that there is abundance for you and for everyone else.

Today see the abundance in the world. Be thankful for all that you have and be open to receive more.

February 23

"All the world's a stage,
And all the men and women merely players.
They have their exits and their entrances,
And one man in his time plays many parts..."
~ William Shakespeare

What roles are you playing?

Do these roles benefit you and those around you?

Some roles such as daughter, son, mother, father, aunt, uncle, cousin, etc. are roles you can't change, but others roles you can change. Are you playing the role of someone who always has to be right? Are you playing the role of a bossy person? A victim? A complainer? You can change these types of roles whenever you want. If a role no longer serves you, change it or drop it. Then take on new roles to become the person you want to be.

Changing who you are can take work, but you can replace old habits and old ways of thinking with new habits and new ways of thinking that will enrich your life and the lives of those around you.

Love the people you are with, but never allow someone to hold you back, and be sure the roles you are playing are ones that lift you up and enrich your life and the lives of those around you.

Today be true to yourself, and whatever roles you play on this stage we call life, play each part with love.

February 24

"I, not events, have the power to make me happy or unhappy today. I can choose which it shall be. Yesterday is dead, tomorrow hasn't arrived yet. I have just one day, today, and I'm going to be happy in it."~ Groucho Marx

Focus on this moment. Be happy in this moment. You decide how you feel. For most people this is not a conscious decision, but it can be. You can decide to stop letting your feelings be controlled by your environment and decide to be happy. Let go of the past, focus on this moment, and the future will take care of itself.

Stop giving your power to the events in your life. You have the ability to decide how you feel. Take control of your life and your emotions, and decide to be happy and peaceful.

Today decide to be happy regardless of what happens. Commit to this fully and what happens may just amaze you.

February 25

"All that we are is the result of what we have thought. It is founded upon our thoughts. It is made up of our thoughts." ~ Buddha

If this is true, and I believe it is, then the only way to change your life is to change your thoughts.

Is there an area of your life that is not exactly as you wish it would be? Is there a problem that keeps coming up? What are your thoughts about that subject? Examine your thoughts and take the time to think of new ideas that will help you. Come up with three short thoughts. If your problem is money you could use:

"It's okay to be rich."
"I can be rich and still be a nice person."
"I enjoy being rich."

After you have the new ideas, spend two minutes every morning and write the ideas on a piece of paper. Then carry the paper with you all day and look at the thoughts when you can. The next morning rewrite the thoughts on a new piece of paper, and continue to do this every day.

By introducing these new thoughts to your consciousness, your brain will at some point accept them and your life will change. Isn't your life worth two minutes a day? Do this every day and do not let any excuse stop you.

Today think about the new you.

February 26

"Love is the ability and willingness to allow those that you care for to be what they choose for themselves without any insistence that they satisfy you." ~ Wayne Dyer

When you love someone, you allow him to be himself. Love is not telling someone he must be a certain way for you to be happy. But by all means if someone does something you don't like, tell him. You can even tell him that if his dangerous behavior continues, you will no longer be a part of his life. If a friend is an alcoholic, you don't need to spend time with him, but if he needs or wants your help, be there for him and still love him.

These are the extremes. In most cases people are not endangering you or themselves, so just allow them to be who they want to be. What you want and what is best for you may not be best for someone else. Give up the idea of changing others and just love people for who they are. When you decide to accept people for who they are where they are, much of the stress and anxiety will leave your life.

Today try to not force your opinion or your will on others.

February 27

"Laughter is an instant vacation."~ Milton Berle

Are you stressed? Worried? Concerned? Angry? Frustrated? You can take a break from your negative world with a smile, and when you laugh you will be transported to a new state of being.

Try this now. Smile. Not the fake smile you used for your school pictures but a real smile. Think of something funny. Try to relive a funny event. Laugh. Even if it isn't a real laugh at first, laugh out loud. Soon you will be laughing for real. Then think of how you feel. Doesn't it feel good? Don't *you* feel good? You can feel like this whenever you want. These good feelings are always inside you. All you need to do is let them out.

Today remember to laugh.

February 28

"While I know myself as a creation of God, I am also obligated to realize and remember that everyone else and everything else is also God's creation."~ Maya Angelou

Most people would agree there is a Divine Creator or God who created our world and everything in it. So when we look at the world and the people in it, it is like looking at a painting by a great master. The painting reflects the painter, not all of the painter, but a glimpse into who the painter is.

The Bible tells us that God is love, so when we look at the world, we see all of the ways that love can express itself. We may not understand why things happen, just like we may not understand all of the nuances in the painting, but know that it is all God expressing himself. Then when you look in the mirror, know that you are God expressing herself as love.

Today see the love in everything.

February 29

"Not what we have, but what we enjoy, constitutes our abundance."~ Epicurus

Have you ever heard the stories of people who live life in poverty and when they die their relatives find they had millions of dollars? I don't know if these stories are true, but I do know there are many people who do not enjoy what they have.

When you don't enjoy what you have, you tend to look for new things to enjoy. Learn to enjoy what you currently possess. You don't need the newest gadget. You don't need another toy. It is likely that you would be better served by getting rid of some of the stuff you have now.

When you make use of what you have, you are in the flow of abundance. When your stuff is sitting useless, the flow has stopped. Get rid of the stuff you don't use, and use what you have.

Today enjoy what you have.

March 1
"Judge not, that you be not judged."~ Jesus Christ

Judging is part of what we do as people. It is part of the decision making process. But when we judge other people, we limit them from becoming more than they are in this moment. In other words, if someone does something that you believe hurts you, you may judge that person as bad and never allow the goodness inside him to shine in your eyes.

When you accept people as they are without judgement, then you can decide if you want them in your life without having to first label them as good or bad. When you allow people to be themselves, you will be open to the greatness of the world. When you accept people as they are, you free yourself from the pettiness and triviality that often accompanies judgement.

Today limit your judgements and accept everyone just as he is.

March 2

"Adopt the pace of nature: her secret is patience."
~ Ralph Waldo Emerson

Patience is a wonderful thing. It's almost impossible to be patient and stressed at the same time. Stress causes more pain, discomfort, and illness than anything else in this world, and patience is the cure.

It is okay to be second, it is okay to sit at a traffic light, and it is okay to wait. When you learn to be patient, the world just seems to fall into place.

Before you do something, just sit for thirty seconds and do nothing. In fact, frequently throughout your day, just sit for thirty seconds and breathe. Try to slow your life down, and you will see patience grow and stress melt away. My only word of caution is that if you decide to become more patient, the universe may send you opportunities to practice your patience. Stick with it. It is worth it, and when you are truly patient, the tests will be easy.

Today be patient.

March 3

"Your present circumstances don't determine where you can go; they merely determine where you start."~ Nido Qubein

When you learn to accept this, your life can change. You must accept where you are and then decide where you want to be. Only then can you decide how to get there. Many people are either unclear about where they want to go or unrealistic about where they are.

Be honest with yourself about your situation. You can get to where you would like to be, but you must first accept where you are. Then devise a plan to get to where you want to go. And here is a secret - the bigger the goal, the less important your starting point.

If your goal is to be the richest person in the world, you will need $60,000,000,000. If you are totally broke, you will need to make all of the sixty billion dollars to reach your goal. If you already have $1,000,000, you will still need to get $59,999,000,000 to reach your goal. The difference between these two amounts is less than 1/100th of 1%.

Put another way, if the grocery store is ten miles due west of your house but only five miles due west of your friend's house, that may seem like a big difference. However, if you live on the East Coast and are planning a trip to California, whether you leave from your house or your friend's house is really insignificant. Remember, the farther you want to go, the less important your starting point. So set big goals and have big dreams.

Today decide where you want to be and start moving in that direction.

March 4

"The day you are happy for no reason whatsoever, the day you find yourself taking delight in everything and in nothing, you will know that you have found the land of unending joy called the kingdom."~ Anthony deMello

Anthony deMello was saying that the kingdom (of heaven) is at hand. You can have heaven on earth by being happy for no reason. True happiness is uncaused. True happiness is found by letting go of the things that are preventing you from being happy.

You are like a swimmer who has heavy weights strapped to you. You can try to swim harder to keep your head above water, or you can just let go of the weights. The more weight you let go of, the easier it is to keep your head above water. Your anger, resentments, and judgements are weighing you down. As you let them go of them, it will be easier to experience happiness.

Today stop looking for things to make you happy. Just let go of the things that are preventing your happiness from coming out.

March 5

"If you correct your mind, the rest of your life will fall into place."~ Lao Tzu

Before you spend lots of time and energy trying to change something in your life, first change your mindset. Think thoughts of health, wealth, and happiness, and then take action. If your thoughts are not in line with what you desire, you will sabotage yourself.

When thoughts that are not in agreement with your desires come into your mind, replace them with the thoughts you want. Affirm that what you desire is on the way and be grateful for it. Replace thoughts of lack, want, and sickness with thoughts of health, gratitude, and abundance. Then get to work on making your dreams a reality.

Today think grand wonderful thoughts.

March 6

"You cannot find yourself by going into the past. You can find yourself by coming into the present."~ Eckhart Tolle

Our perception of the past is not accurate. We think about the events of the past, and they are clouded by our judgement and our opinion. The past is an illusion. When we want to find who we truly are, the only place to look is right here, right now.

Why would you want to know who you truly are? When you know your true Self, you can act and think in line with that Self. When I speak of Self, I mean the you that is connected with the Divine Creator. When you know who you truly are, you will know that connection and act from that.

Right here, right now ask yourself, what is my highest good? What can I do right now to express my true nature? What am I here to do? The answers you get may change from day to day because you are changing and evolving. So live in this moment and express your true Self in this moment.

Today let the greatest grandest version of you come out.

March 7

"To be wronged is nothing unless you continue to remember it."~ Confucius

What does it mean to be wronged? For me it means that someone has done something that affects me that I judged as wrong. The other person didn't think it was wrong or she wouldn't have done it. She may have known that I wouldn't like it, but she had to see some benefit in doing it. So the easiest way for me to get over it is to change my judgement. When I no longer view the event as being wrong, it is much easier to let it go.

Think about a time when you were wronged. Try to understand the other person's point of view. Then forgive her and forgive yourself for judging her. The more you do this the more you will be free of the past.

Today just let go.

March 8

"The qualities we respect in adults we repress in children."
~ Mark Rose

This first hit me when my daughter was in kindergarten. The most successful adults break the rules, think differently than the norm, are often disruptive, take risks, and tell people how they really feel. When kids in school do these things they get in trouble. So how can we teach our children not to get in trouble but still retain their creative and independent spirit?

I think part of the secret is teaching them respect. You are quiet in class out of respect for the other students, not because the rules say to be quiet. And when rules do not make any sense, teach your children to question them. They should learn that sometimes there will be people in authority who make bad decisions and silly rules.

Teach your children to question authority when they disagree with it. I realize this may result in more trips to the principal's office, but I would rather have a child who can make decisions and stand up for his or her rights than a sheep who follows the crowd.

Teach your children not to follow the crowd. Teach them to think for themselves. Teach them to listen to their gut instincts and follow their hearts. But above all, teach them to do everything with love.

Today teach your children to be extraordinary.

March 9

"There can be no real freedom without the freedom to fail."
~ Erich Fromm

Often people are paralyzed by the fear of failure. A countless number of businesses never get started, thousands of books never get written, and millions of experiences never get experienced all because of fear. The truly ironic thing is that the simplest way to fail is to never start.

If you have thought about writing a book, but you are afraid it won't be good enough, you'll probably never start writing it. By facing your fear and writing the book, you at least have the chance of it getting published. By staying stuck in fear, you are guaranteed to fail.

Try facing your fear and doing something you have wanted to do but thought you couldn't. You may not be able to finish the task, but there is also the chance that you will go farther than you ever imagined. You will never know unless you start.

Today start something amazing.

March 10

"The more tranquil a man becomes, the greater is his success, his influence, his power for good. Calmness of mind is one of the beautiful jewels of wisdom."~ James Allen

There are times when I know that raising my voice will do a better job of getting my daughter's attention than talking in a normal tone. However, I do this only for effect. I am not angry, and I remain calm on the inside. Staying calm allows me to make clear decisions. It also allows me to react to anger and fear in others with love, defusing situations instead of escalating them.

There are times when excitement and emotion can be used for effect, but it is helpful to stay calm on the inside. If you notice yourself getting angry or aggravated, do your best to calm down. When you are calm, you will do a much better job of dealing with the situation.

Today stay calm.

March 11

"God gave you a gift of 86,400 seconds today. Have you used one to say thank you?"~ William A. Ward

Find something every day to be grateful for. You are very blessed. Take the time to acknowledge that. Take the time to thank the people in your life. Take the time to appreciate all that you have. The more you are thankful for, the more you will find to be thankful for.

Today be thankful.

March 12

"If you are in peace you are in a position of power."
~ Joel Osteen

There is a difference between power and force. Force creates a reaction. Force is moving against something. Power is at rest. Power does not create a reaction against anything. When you are at peace, you are not exerting force on anyone or anything, so there are no reactive forces acting on you. In stillness your power is allowed to grow, and you realize that you have all that you need. When you are in a place of power, the world will conform to give you what is best for you.

Ghandi was a great example of power without force. He never forced anything. He stated the desires and wants of his people and waited for them to happen. His power came, not from his millions of followers, but from his trust in God. His name for God may have been Brahman, but the name is not important, the faith is.

Today stop trying to force things and be at peace.

March 13

"Racism isn't born, folks, it's taught. I have a two-year-old son. You know what he hates? Naps! End of list."
~ Denis Leary

Scientists tell us the only two fears we are born with are the fear of falling and the fear of loud noises. Every other fear and every other prejudice is learned. When we hate anything, we are blocking joy and blessings. If you hate mornings, you will likely never enjoy a sunrise. If you hate a group or a race of people, then you are missing the opportunity to know many wonderful people. Judging the character of many based on the actions of just a few is a hard way to live. Before you judge a group or a race of people, think about the people in your own group. Is there anyone in your group who thinks and acts differently than you?

Many times we get our fears and our hatreds from our parents. Stop this cycle now. Let go of your fears and hatreds and replace them with kindness. Show your children how to respect everyone.

Today be extraordinarily kind to someone you would usually fear or hate. And if you do not fear or hate anyone, just be kind and take a nap.

March 14
"All forgiveness is self forgiveness."~ Wayne Dyer

By not forgiving, you are filling yourself with negative emotion. Forgive everyone for everything and free yourself from the pain.

When you forgive, you open your heart to love, beauty, and the Divine. Let the past go and move on. Stop punishing yourself for the actions of others.

By forgiving them, you also forgive yourself for judging another Divine perfect creation.

Today forgive just one person, and tomorrow forgive one more.

March 15
"Happiness doesn't depend upon who you are or what you have; it depends solely on what you think."~ Dale Carnegie

If happiness were dependent on location, than everyone would want to live in one zip code. Happiness doesn't depend on wealth because there are rich people who are unhappy as well as poor people who are happy.

Dale Carnegie was absolutely correct. Happiness is an inside job.

If an event starts to upset you, start thinking happy thoughts, send love to the person or situation, and watch your world transform. It really is just that simple. Choose to be happy, and you will be happy no matter what happens.

Today think thoughts of happiness and love.

March 16

"Those who bring sunshine into the lives of others cannot keep it from themselves."~ James M. Barrie

Life is about giving. Whatever you give you will get. When you give kindness, you get kindness. When you give love, you get love. You decide what to give and you control your life.

Today be the light of the world, shining your love on everyone you meet.

March 17

"Abundance is not something we acquire. It is something we tune into."~ Wayne Dyer

Abundance is a flow. Abundance is like electricity. You can have a battery, a lot of batteries, or you can plug into the power grid. To tune into abundance, you need to realize that everything comes from God, and God is limitless. God is the power grid of abundance.

Stop looking at the lack that you perceive in your life and in the world. By focusing on the lack, you will experience lack. If you focus on abundance, you will experience abundance. Abundance is always here. It is always around you. You just need to tap into it to experience it.

Look at the abundance in your life. Be grateful for everything you have, and tap into unlimited abundance. Allow abundance to flow, not to you but through you. A flow must keep flowing. As you allow abundance to flow through you, your abundance will increase.

Today stop trying to keep more and let abundance flow.

March 18

"Without passion you don't have energy. Without energy you have nothing."~ Donald Trump

Everything is energy. The more positive energy you can put into something, the better the chance it will do well. The more passion you have, the more positive energy you will have for whatever you are doing.

Think about the things you do in your life. What are you passionate about? Focus on those things. Try to delegate the things you are not passionate about to someone else, or figure out a way that they can become more enjoyable. Attaching a different meaning to those tasks can help with your enthusiasm. You may not be able to get excited about doing the dishes, but if you look at that task as helping your spouse to enjoy the environment of your home, washing the dishes can become a labor of love.

Today focus on your passion and try to infuse every action with passion.

March 19

"Don't lose your peace of mind just because everyone else can't find theirs."~ Steve Jenkins

We often take on the feelings and emotions of the people around us. When someone who's emotionally charged with negative energy walks in a room, it's easy for the other people in the room to take on that emotion. You can prevent this from happening by choosing how you want to feel. You get to choose your emotions. You are in control of how you feel and how you react. You can give away that ability and allow other people to choose your emotions for you, or you can be in control of how you feel.

The next time you're in a situation where someone is freaking out, just remember that you can stay calm. You can stay happy and still help him. Decide right now that you're not willing to give up your peace of mind.

Today decide to be happy.

March 20

"Happiness resides not in possessions and not in gold. Happiness dwells in the soul."~ Democritus

Often people are searching for happiness. They buy things, they move, or they try to find happiness in other people. Many people spend their entire lives looking outside themselves for something that is a part of who they are.

Happiness is not the result of acquiring anything but rather of letting go. You don't become happy when you meet the right person. You become happy when you release the thought that you are incomplete. You don't become happy when you buy the new car. You become happy when you release the need for a new car. You don't become happy when you get the promotion. You become happy when you stop searching for respect.

Stop searching for happiness, and release the need for something more. Let go of your needs. Sure you can strive for more. Sure you can want better things in your life, but learn to be happy right here and right now.

Today release the need for something else in your life and just accept happiness now.

March 21

"We can never obtain peace in the outer world until we make peace with ourselves."~ Dalai Lama

Peace and happiness are very similar. If you are not at peace, you will not find peace in the world. The peace you desire is within your grasp. You only need to look within yourself to find it. When you have decided to embrace your inner peace, your outer world will become more peaceful.

When you allow your inner peace to come through, your world becomes peaceful and you experience happiness. You can start by letting go. Let go of your attachment to something and see how you become more at peace. Let go of expectations and desires. Remember the only place for peace to start is inside you. Your peace must begin with you, and my peace must begin with me.

Today embrace your inner peace.

March 22

"Things turn out best for the people who make the best of the way things turn out."~ Ty Boyd

In other words, it isn't what happens, but how you react to what happens that matters. When events occur in your life, find the good. Find the positive in the event. It is always there. When you continue to find the good, the good will be easier to find.

The most successful people find the good in every situation and use every event to their advantage.

Today look for the good.

March 23

"All of the forces in the world are not so powerful as an idea whose time has come."~ Victor Hugo

Ideas have a life of their own, and often ideas are given to several people at once to be sure they come to completion. When an idea gets hold of you, be sure to act on it. A great idea can take you farther than you could ever imagine.

Also, be on the lookout for ideas that other people have. Our world is constantly changing. The people who embrace these changes and learn how to benefit from them will be far ahead of the people who cling to the past.

Today look to the future and create the life you want by embracing new ideas now.

March 24

"A man's true wealth is the good he does in the world."
~ Kahil Gibran

Many great teachers have told us that we are measured not by what we have but by what we give. Several years ago the WWJD (What would Jesus do?) bracelets were popular. Let's ask that question in our lives.

Would Jesus help other people no matter what they believed?

Would Jesus share his love and wisdom with the world?

Would Jesus do everything he could to make the world a better place?

Would Jesus give of his time and his resources?

Yes, indeed. He did do all of these things. Many Christian churches call Jesus the savior. Maybe his way of saving us was to show us how to live. Perhaps his gift to the world was to show everyone the power of giving. At the end of the day ask yourself what you have contributed to make the world a better place.

Today give something that will help the world. Give a smile, give your time, or give love.

March 25

"You cannot teach people anything. You can only help them discover it within themselves."~ Galileo

Within you is love, peace, and happiness. I hope I can help you realize that. And then you can help others realize who they truly are. If you are not experiencing love, peace, and happiness, something is blocking the flow. Examine your life. What is keeping your love from flowing? Remove the blocks and you will experience your divine nature.

One simple step is to say good things about yourself. So many people say negative, self limiting things. Stop doing that and start telling the world you are great. Not egotistically saying you are better than another, but confidently affirming your greatness. Then you can share that with everyone you meet. You can be the light of your world.

Today share your happiness with someone else.

March 26

"The new spirituality is that it will produce an experience in human encounters in which we become a living demonstration of the basic spiritual teaching. We are all one."~ Neale Donald Walsch

If we are all one, then what I do to you, I do to myself. If we are all one, then how I treat you affects me. If we are all one, then we are connected to everything else, and how we treat the planet is how we are treating ourselves. If we are all one, then the best thing for me to do is to love everyone as myself, and that is what Jesus taught.

Jesus taught us to love each other. He never said we should condemn, judge, and exclude others, but that is what many Christians do. You can live your life to be more Christ like, you can love and accept everyone, and you can allow people to believe what they want. Sure you can share your beliefs, but if other people's beliefs are different, that's okay. If they have a different name for God, love them anyway. Give them the love that you would like to receive.

We are all connected, and when you love and accept everyone and everything, you are loving yourself and making the world a more loving place.

Today ask yourself, what would Jesus do? He would love everyone and everything, without exception.

March 27

"Whatever happens, take responsibility." ~ Tony Robbins

The next time you are with some friends and something goes wrong, I want you to say, "This is my fault. I assume 100% responsibility for this, and I will do all I can to fix it." Say that even if the problem is the weather. Then watch what happens.

Most people want to avoid the responsibility for problems. Because of this, they assume the role of victim. When you are the victim, it is easier to say, "It wasn't my fault." But when you take responsibility for the problem, whatever it is, other people will be glad the responsibility is not theirs. Then they are free to focus on a solution, or at least move on.

At work if you are partly or entirely responsible for a problem, just own up to it. Most bosses are smart enough to know that everyone makes mistakes and that the solution is more important than the problem. So when you say, "It is my responsibility, and this is what I am doing to fix it," the boss will be happy that you are moving forward instead of looking backward.

The more you take responsibility, the easier your life will be and the more you will be able to get done.

Today say, "I am responsible," at least once.

March 28

"The only real failure in life is not to be true to the best one knows."~ Buddha

Do you do your best? It is hard to do your best at everything when you are doing five things at once.

Would you go to a surgeon who told you he was going to be performing three operations at once, or would you rather have him focus on just you?

How many pro athletes do you know who compete in different sports?

Are you preventing yourself from doing your best because you are doing so many things? The great people in history are usually known for doing one thing very well.

Focus on the thing that you are best at and do that as well as you can. Then teach your children to do the same. If your child is great at art but bad at math, hire an art tutor to nourish her gifts. When she becomes a great artist, then she can hire an accountant.

Today focus on what you do well, and do that to the best of your ability.

March 29

"Nothing but your own thoughts can hamper your progress."
~ *A Course in Miracles*

Everything humans ever created was first a thought. The Great Wall of China, The Pyramids at Giza, the cereal you had for breakfast, all began as thoughts. No stones were laid, no cows milked, nothing happened before it was a thought. Your progress on the road of life is a result of your thoughts, and your thoughts determine your actions. You choose if you want to think thoughts that will help your progress or hinder your progress, and your thoughts alone will determine your journey.

There will be times when a limiting thought pops into your head. Change it to a positive thought. Replace your thoughts of lack and limitation with thoughts of abundance and gratitude. Repeat the positive idea ten times in your mind to erase the negative thought. Soon the positive thoughts will dominate your thinking.

Today decide to think thoughts that help you.

March 30

"When someone offends you, you can raise your spirits to heights where offenses cannot reach."~ Anthony deMello

Are you letting other people control your emotions? When you get mad at something someone said or did, you are giving that person control over you. This goes for good or bad. When you feel good because of something someone said or did, you can also feel bad because of something he said or did. Don't be a puppet. Don't let other people pull your strings.

You can move above this. You can choose to be happy no matter what other people say or do. You can choose to rise above what most people consider normal. You can take control of your emotions and your life.

Today live in a state of happiness no matter what happens.

March 31

"Develop an attitude of gratitude and give thanks for everything that happens to you, knowing that every step forward is a step toward achieving something bigger and better than your current situation."~ Brian Tracy

By giving thanks for everything in your life, you are able to move away from excuses. If every event is a blessing, and you have no excuses, then there is nothing to keep you from moving toward your goals. When you are grateful for everything in your life, it is easy to move forward. With gratitude you can focus on the positive. You can see the good in everything.

Success can be defined as a progressive realization of a worthy goal. By feeling gratitude for everything, you become successful. Gratitude keeps you moving in the right direction.

Today be grateful for everything.

April 1

"Wise people learn when they can. Fools learn when they must."~ Arthur Wellesley, 1st Duke of Wellington

Continuing education has been a buzz word in big business for years. Many people are forced to learn more to keep up to date with their jobs. Do you learn just when you have to, or do you learn because learning is fun? There is so much information in books, audio books, and the internet, that if you spent every waking minute learning for the rest of your life, you would still never learn a fraction of what there is to learn. No one is going to do that, but could you spend an hour a day? How about half an hour? If you spent just thirty minutes a day reading or listening to audio books, you would read a book about every two weeks, or about twenty-five books a year. How much better would you be at your job, or as a parent, or just at living if you read twenty-five books a year? How about fifty books a year?

Listening to audio books in your car is a great way to maximize your time. Other possibilities are to cut out one hour of TV in the evening or to get up a little earlier in the morning. If you're serious about learning, you'll find the time each day to do it. The more you learn, the better off you will be.

Today expand your mind. Learn something.

April 2

"Your most precious, valued possessions and your greatest powers are invisible and intangible. No one can take them. You, and you alone, can give them. You will receive abundance for your giving."~ W. Clement Stone

Your most precious possession is love. Nothing you can give is more valuable or more essential. Give love and you will get love. When you give love it can be in any form. It could be a new invention the world has been waiting for, or a service, or a hug, or it could simply be a smile. When you give love, the grace of the angels will shine down upon you.

Today give love.

April 3

"Your success and happiness lie in you. Resolve to keep happy, and your joy and you shall form an invincible host against difficulties."~ Helen Keller

Happiness and success are both inside you. Success is a state of mind. There are millionaires who view themselves as not having reached the level of success they want, and janitors who consider themselves hugely successful. Others may look at your life and judge you and your success, but that should have no influence on your view of yourself.

When you decide to accept where you are right now, that is happiness. When you are moving toward a worthwhile goal, that is success. You decide the goal and the rate of movement, and since those are your choices, your success is up to you. Your goal may be to attain great wealth, to clean the building in which you work, or to spread peace in the world. As long as the goal is worthwhile to you, move in that direction and enjoy your success.

Today decide to be happy and successful.

April 4

"The greatest obstacle to discovery is not ignorance-it is the illusion of knowledge."~ Daniel J. Boorstin

When we think we know all there is to know, we stop searching for the answer. For 100,000 years human flight was thought to be impossible. There was no reason for people to try to build a plane because they already knew it was not possible. Now flying is commonplace. Cell phones were once just a sci-fi myth and so was video conferencing and 3D printing.

Many of the things that are common to us now were thought to be impossible 100 years ago. What will be possible in the next 100 years? What beliefs of yours have changed over the years? What did you once believe to be true that now you know is not true? What did you think was impossible that is now possible? The world we live in is constantly changing, and so are you. Look at your life and imagine if the things you know to be true were no longer true. How would do things differently? What would you dare to do?

Today cast off the illusion of knowledge and let your imagination run wild.

April 5

"The constant assertion of belief is an indication of fear."
~ Jiddu Krishnamurti

Often when people are trying to convince you of something, they are also trying to convince themselves. Although this is not always the case, it can be. People who are sure of their beliefs are not threatened when someone else believes differently.

If someone told you you had blue skin, would it upset you? Would you try to prove them wrong or just think they were nuts? You'd think they're nuts because you know you don't have blue skin. Now what if someone said you were fat and you actually believe you are overweight. Would you come up with excuses and defend yourself? That defense is the fear that they are right.

What are you defending yourself against? What comments create the biggest reaction in you? Why do you believe these things, and can you change your beliefs? Look at what upsets you. Those are the things you are afraid of. Send love to those fears and watch them disappear.

Today don't defend yourself when someone says something about you. Allow them to have their opinion and move on.

April 6

"No one has ever hurt or upset you."~ Anthony deMello

I realize you may not believe this, so let me explain.

John Smith's car was stolen. Did this news upset you? Now imagine your car was stolen. Would this upset you? The event is the same - a car got stolen. The difference is you put more importance on your car than John Smith's car, so when your car is stolen it generates an emotional response. However, the emotional response is a choice you make.

You decide how to react to every event in your life. Your reaction or response is what causes you pain or upset, not the event. The event is just a set of facts, and the facts are neutral. You don't see them as neutral, however, when you perceive them as good or bad.

The Earth has a gravitational field that pulls everything on the surface of the planet down. I realize this isn't very scientific, but you get the idea. Gravity exists and most of us don't think about it. Now imagine you are bungee jumping. Gravity just became fun. Or imagine you just fell out of a tree. Gravity just became bad. Gravity didn't change. Your perception changed.

You can decide if you are going to get upset or not. The decision is up to you. When you give away that power and let other people choose your mood, you may not like their choices.

Today keep your power and choose to be happy.

April 7

"There is no security on this earth. There is only opportunity." ~ Douglas MacArthur

Many people are searching for security. They want a safe job or a safe relationship, but safety is an illusion. Thousands of people at Enron thought they had safe jobs. People in safe relationships may one day find themselves alone.

Having a good job and loving relationships is great but only when you know that you are complete within yourself. Only when you know that you have the ability to walk away from a job can you truly enjoy it. When you are tied to a job or a person you have decided you can't live without, you are a prisoner, and the thing that holds you prisoner can't love you and you can't truly love it.

When your self identity and self worth come from outside of yourself, there is always a chance that your world will fall apart. When your self worth comes from inside of you, then the outside world has less influence over you, and only then can you be secure. Your security is not from the world but from you.

Opportunities are often hidden in problems. However, when you are secure in yourself, it is much easier to act on those opportunities.

Today be confident and secure from within yourself and look for the opportunities.

April 8
"If it feels good do it."~ Unknown

I love this statement. I am not promoting a hedonistic lifestyle, although if that's what you want then go for it. I think of how things feel emotionally not physically. When you eat the second bowl of ice cream it may be physically satisfying, but if you have regret and guilt after finishing it, that feels bad. If while shopping, you see a big screen TV that looks great but know you'll stress over paying the credit card bill when it comes in, then don't buy the TV.

Your emotions are your guide. When you are feeling happiness, joy, love, gratitude, or forgiveness, then you are in line with your true self. When you are feeling anger, fear, resentment, greed, or illness, you are not in line with your true self.

When you feel negative emotions, the key is first to recognize them and then release them. Let go of whatever it is you are holding onto that is making you feel bad. And finally try to avoid similar situations in the future.

Today just feel good.

April 9

"My religion is very simple. My religion is kindness."
~ Dalai Lama

Be kind to everyone and everything you encounter in your life. Sometimes this may be difficult, but kindness becomes easier if you don't judge. When you can accept every person and every situation just the way it is, then kindness will easily flow from you.

Kindness is simple. We can all be kind. Even when a person or situation is not what you wanted or expected, you can still be kind. Imagine what the world would be like if everyone were kind to everyone else all of the time. That is the dream of peace on Earth, and it starts with you. You have no control over what other people do, but you can control your thoughts and actions.

Today choose to be kind, and you will be amazed at how your life can transform.

April 10

"I am responsible for my world. If I want peace in my world, I need to change the only thing I can change - me. If I am at peace then my world will be peaceful."~ Mark Rose

Peace is the inner knowing that the world is working perfectly and that everything is exactly as it should be. When you can get to that point in your life, the troubles of the world will no longer be seen as troubles. Problems will become events which you no longer need to judge as bad or wrong.

All of the great masters have done this, and you can too. See everything as a perfect Divine creation. Don't judge events as right or wrong. Just look at the facts, step back, and look at the event without comparing it to events from your past. Bring peace and love to situations that used to cause you stress or apprehension.

Know that by being free of judgement, every event can be one of peace and love. See the good in all that happens, and when you can't actually see the good, at least know that it is there. Know that the Divine forces are conspiring to do you good. Think this and live this. Make this part of your everyday experience, and your life will become more peaceful. Peace truly does begin with each of us because there is no other place it can begin.

Today choose to be at peace, avoid judgement, accept the world as it is, and be in the now.

April 11

"If you're not happy with what you've got, then why do you want more?"~ Wayne Dyer

All that you have and all that you are is a result of what you have thought. Your thoughts have influenced your decisions and actions. Your decisions and actions give you the results you have. Stop wishing for more. If you do not like what you have been getting, start changing your thoughts.

Think thoughts of where you would like to be. Set a goal. Then before you make a decision, ask yourself if the action you are about to take will help you move toward your goal or not. Make decisions that help move you toward your goal.

Today set your goal. Then do something every day to move you in the direction of the goal. You can make time for this to happen. Just turn off your ELDD (electronic life diminishing device. You may know this as a television).

April 12

"Perhaps the very best question that you can memorize and repeat, over and over is, what is the most valuable use of my time right now?"~ Brian Tracy

Throughout the day it is easy to get distracted and off task. I have found that a "to do" list helps keep me on task, but I still like this question. I even have it hanging on the wall above my desk.

When you ask yourself this question throughout the day, you will make better use of your time. If you have written goals, you can also ask yourself if the task you are doing is moving you closer to your goals. The more time you spend moving toward your goals, the sooner you will reach them.

Einstein, Edison, Da Vinci, Mozart, and all of the great people throughout history had the same amount of time in each day as you do. The difference is how they used their time.

Today use your time wisely because you can never recover wasted time.

April 13
"Be more concerned with your character than your reputation because your character is what you really are, while your reputation is merely what others think you are."
~ John Wooden

I think the key word in this quote is "merely." "Your reputation is *merely* what others think you are." Mr. Wooden is saying that your character is vitally important, while your reputation is insignificant. It is not just that character is more important, but rather that what others think of you has little or no value.

Abraham Lincoln said, "You can't please all of the people all of the time," so stop trying. Do what you think is right, what you think is best, and don't concern yourself with the opinions of others. A person's opinion of you is the result of his history as much as your actions, and since his history is out of your control, so is his opinion.

The people who have had the most impact on the world always went against the common thinking. They always did things that were different. Stop worrying about what other people think about you, and do what is yours to do.

Today do what you think is best.

April 14

"The greatest accomplishment is not in never falling, but in rising again after you fall."~ Vince Lombardi

Anyone who has never failed has never tried. Try something now so you can fail and get it out of the way. When you realize that failing is not as bad as you feared, get up and try something new.

Babe Ruth led the league in strike outs and Michael Jordan missed more shots than he made. Both of these men were hugely successful, but only because they kept trying. They focused on their successes and not their failures. When they missed they tried again, and again, and again.

Today don't be afraid to fail at something. Then try something new.

April 15

"The truest greatness lies in being kind, the truest wisdom in a happy mind."~ Ella Wheeler Wilcox

Be kind and happy. Happiness usually flows with kindness. When you give kindness, you get kindness in return, not because the person you were kind to will be nice to you, although that is likely to happen, but because the universe will return to you what you give away. When you are kind to others, kindness will return to you.

When you decide to be happy, you will be. When you decide to let go of the things that are keeping you from being happy, your happiness will flow, and the wisdom of the universe will be yours.

Today decide to be kind and happy.

April 16

"It's the job that's never started that takes longest to finish."
~ J. R. R. Tolkien

This seems so obvious, but think about the truth of it in your own life. Is there a job you wish were finished, but you haven't even started it yet? Do you look at your garage and say, "I need to clean this up"? Then months go by and the garage is still a mess? If you worked on it for just five minutes a day, after a month you would have put in two and a half hours. How about if you worked on it for ten minutes a day? Or fifteen?

How you use your time is up to you, but if you want to finish something, you need to start it first.

Today start that project you have been meaning to finish.

April 17

"There is no inherent meaning in information. It's what we do with that information that matters."~ Beau Lotto

We often have trouble separating the facts from our opinion of the facts. Our brains work so quickly that when we hear a fact we instantly assign a meaning to that fact. This is a great tool that allows us to assess situations quickly. However, we often assign a meaning that does not help us, and the line between the fact and the meaning disappears.

Here is an example. If your name is Abel Kirui and today is April 5, 2009, you just ran the fastest marathon in your life while posting one of the ten fastest marathon times in history, 2h5m:4s, and you finished in third place. That you ran the marathon in 2h5m:4s is a fact. That you are happy because you did your best and posted one of the fastest times ever, or that you are disappointed because you didn't win is a choice. You determine the meaning you give to the facts. Are you comparing yourself to others, or are you comparing yourself to who you were yesterday?

Think about the events in your life and the meanings you have given them. Can you give them a different meaning? Would a new meaning serve you better? Can you remove the meaning altogether?

Today remember the facts are neutral.

April 18

"Miracles are simply a change in perception."
~ Mark Victor Hansen

Our perception is a result of our beliefs. What we believe determines how we see the world and the people in it. Our beliefs are what we use to decide if a fact or an event is good or bad. The facts are always neutral. Only our beliefs or perceptions determine good or bad.

You can look at the world as if everything is a miracle and is here for your good, or you can choose to see the opposite. The choice is yours. When you see the world as loving, and you can see the love in every situation, then you are open to miracles in your life.

Today choose to see miracles. Choose to live from love.

April 19

"Life is very short, and there's no time for fussing and fighting my friend."~ The Beatles

I had lunch today with two friends, both of whom have been diagnosed with cancer within the last twelve months. One is undergoing chemo treatments, and the other is through his treatments and is in remission.

When I think about this line from the Beatles, and I think about my friends, it reminds me of what is really important in life. Spending time with the people I love is very high on that list, but so is loving the people that I happen to be spending time with.

Life can be hectic and busy with meetings and responsibilities, but take the time to keep connected to the people you care about, even if it's just a phone call. And if there is someone from whom you have drifted away, or if you have had a feud that has lasted for years, today may be the day to put that aside and mend that relationship. Do what feels right to you. Relationships take time and effort, but there is no greater way to spend your energy. Make sure the people you love know how you feel.

Today connect with at least one person you haven't seen lately.

April 20

"You have no cause for anything but gratitude and joy."
~ Buddha

Be thankful for everything in your life, without exception. I am sure you have heard, "Everything that doesn't kill you makes you stronger." But that isn't exactly true. Every event has the potential to be a blessing. Your reaction to the event determines if it is a blessing or not.

If you get charged with a DUI, it may be the wake up call you needed to let you know you drink too much. You can be grateful for the opportunity to reclaim your life, or you can deny that you have a problem and keep drinking. If you do have a problem, the universe will keep sending you situations that indicate it is time for you to change your lifestyle. You get to choose if you want to change or not. You get to choose to see the DUI as something to be thankful for or something to be mad about.

Look at your life. What are you mad about? What isn't going the way you would like it to go? Is the world sending you a message? Is there something you could change that would change your life? If there is something in your life that you are not thankful for, ask yourself what you would do differently if you looked at that situation as a blessing. You have the power to change your life, and it starts with gratitude.

Today be grateful and full of joy.

April 21

"I was told to challenge every spiritual teacher, every world leader to utter the one sentence that no religion, no political party, and no nation on the face of the earth will dare utter: 'Ours is not a better way, ours is merely another way.'"
~ Neale Donald Walsch

I try to share this message as much as I can. I know that my beliefs, what I share with you, work for me, but I don't know if they work for you. I can share insights and truths as I know them, but you have to walk your own path.

All paths lead to God. Some are easier. Some are harder. Some are shorter. Some are longer. We each have our own path. I hope that I have made your path easier, and I hope that your journey is filled with peace and love.

Remember this when you meet another traveler. His journey may take him to places where you do not wish to go. But he is on the path that's right for him. It's not our job to judge the journey of another, but to just keep making progress as we go along.

Today enjoy your journey and allow others to enjoy their journeys.

April 22

"Be the change you wish to see in the world."~ Gandhi

Have you ever looked for the How to Fix Other People section in your local book store? Is isn't there, but if it were, it would be very popular. Many people believe that their problems are all because of other people, and if those other people would just change, then their life would be perfect. Have you ever thought that? In the past I have, but no longer. I am here to tell you that your problems are just that, your problems, and if you want your problems to go away, then you need to change the only thing you can change. YOU.

If you want the people in your life to be more polite, then you need to be more polite. If you want your in-laws to treat you with love and respect, then you need to treat them with love and respect. If you want the world to see you for the beautiful, perfect, Divine creation you are, then you need to see the world for the beautiful, perfect, Divine creation it is. The world and the people in it will mirror you. Every great religious tradition tells us this. Stop trying to change the world. Change yourself and your world will change.

You may think I am trying to get you to change, but that is not the case. I believe you are perfect. If, however, you would like to see changes in your world, this is one path to the new world you are looking for. If you are happy with your life the way it is, congratulations and keep up the good work.

Today be the person you want your children to become.

April 23

"If you deliberately plan on being less than you are capable of being, then I warn you that you'll be unhappy for the rest of your life."~ Abraham Maslow

Be all you can be. Push yourself to do your best, and you will be happy as long as you remember one thing. Let go of your expectation of results.

When you run a race, if you do your best and you come in third, you will be happy knowing that you did everything you could. However, if you come in third and know that you could have done better, you may never forgive yourself.

Do your best and let the results be what they may. Let go of your attachment to the outcome and just do your best.

Today be all you can be. Be happy.

April 24

"You can complain because roses have thorns, or you can rejoice because thorns have roses."~ Ziggy, comic strip character created by Tom Wilson

You can look at any situation by focusing on the bad or the good. You can be upset because your plane is delayed, or you can be happy that the problem with the plane was found before takeoff. We are conditioned to look for the bad when things do not go as we would like them to, but I would challenge you to look for the good. It's always there. And if you can't find the good in a situation, find the good in the rest of your life. Think about all of the blessings in your life, and then the situation that you think is bad won't seem so bad.

Focus on the good until doing so becomes a habit. The more you focus on the good, the easier it will be to find it everywhere.

Today focus on the good.

April 25

"You are rewarded not according to your work or your time but according to the measure of your love."~ Saint Catherine

Have you ever wondered why some people work very hard but never get anywhere? Some people always have problems, and just when they start to make some progress, something happens and they get pushed down. Or have you ever known someone who seems to have the luck of the Irish or the Midas touch, a person the world is conspiring to help?

The difference is love. When you send love out into the world, the world sends love back to you. If this concept were difficult to understand, it would be more believable, but this is it. Send love, get love. Send anger, get anger. Whatever you give you get.

Today send love.

April 26

"Men do not attain that which they want but that which they are."~ James Allen

This is the reason the law of attraction is not effective for some people. When your intent is to meet the perfect person and fall in love, but you view yourself as lonely, you will never meet that person and you will continue to experience being lonely.

If we become what we are, then to become rich you must believe you are rich. When you desire to have money, then you are, in essence saying, "I am poor," and you will remain poor. You must feel the feelings of being rich, happy, in love, or at peace to make those experiences come into your life.

Today spend five minutes visioning yourself as having the experience you wish to have.

April 27
"Time you enjoy wasting was not wasted."~ John Lennon

Time is what your life is made of. When you enjoy the time you spend, you are enjoying life, and what is better than enjoying life?

When you learn to enjoy every moment of your life, you will have a great life. Enjoying work and enjoying play are both important. When you are at work, focus on your work. When you are at play, focus on playing. When you are relaxing or having fun, be there fully. Don't think about things you should be doing. Just focus on having fun.

Today enjoy your time no matter what you are doing.

April 28

"If your willingness to give blessings is limited, so is your ability to receive them."~ Lao Tzu

Be willing to give all of the things that you want to get. Give love. Give peace. Give happiness. Give money. But most importantly, give blessings. So many great people in history have told us this, but most people are still trying to get something. When you give up the idea of getting and you start giving, you will get more. And having more will allow you to give more.

God has given us all that we have, so when you give, you are being more God-like. The world was not formed by taking but by giving, so if you want your world to look better, give more.

Today give blessings to everyone.

April 29

"If you're remarkable, it's likely that some people won't like you."~ Seth Godin

If you are remarkable, you must be doing something different than the norm. This will scare some people and inspire others. The ones you scare will not like you. The ones you inspire will love you.

Remember this as you take on something new. If some people are scared of you, and others love you, it is likely because you are doing something great. Focus on the ones who love you, and move beyond the ones who are scared.

94

Today be remarkable and remember that it is okay if everyone doesn't like you.

April 30

"Our ultimate freedom is the right and power to decide how anybody or anything outside ourselves will affect us."
~ Stephen Covey

For most people there are events in their lives that they don't like. The key to happiness is deciding how those events will affect your life. You have the choice of getting upset, and you also have the choice of deciding how long you are going to stay upset. Or, you can choose to stay happy.

When events happen, when people act in a way that you don't like, let go and accept those things for what they are - the past. You can't change the past. You can learn from the past, but don't live there. Learn to let go of your resentment and anger and enjoy this moment.

Today know that you, and only you, have the power to decide how you will feel.

May 1

"There is no duty we so underrate as the duty of being happy. By being happy we sow anonymous benefits upon the world."
~ Robert Louis Stevenson

The only way to have a happy world is to have happy people. There is only one person you can make happy, and that is you. When you are happy, you brighten the world, and you remind the people you meet that they can be happy too.

Today do your part to make the world a happier place. Accept happiness now.

May 2

"Never lose sight of the fact that the most important yardstick of your success will be how you treat other people– your family, friends, and coworkers, and even strangers you meet along the way."~ Barbara Bush

If you have any doubt about this, think about Gandhi, Mother Theresa, and Dr. Martin Luther King Jr. All three of these great leaders taught peace and love, and all three moved mountains. The love you give is not only a great gauge of your life, but also the key to your success.

Try to look at people the way animals do. When you walk into a friend's house, his dog doesn't care if you are wearing an Armani suit or ten year old jeans. The dog just feels your energy. Are you nice or not? When you can treat everyone with love and respect, regardless of his appearance or his station in life, you will be loved and respected.

Today be kind to everyone you meet.

May 3

"Who we understand we love."~ Deepak Chopra

When you understand someone, you can identify with him. You can see yourself in his place doing what he does. You can see yourself in him. When that happens, you love him. That isn't the same as being in love. But when you love someone, your relationship with him can grow and become a wondrous thing of beauty.

The secret is that you are connected to everyone. If you look closely, you will see a part of yourself in every other person. If there is someone you don't like, look for the connection, and watch your love for that person grow.

Today understand everyone.

May 4

"It is better to be a lion for a day than a sheep all your life."
~ Elizabeth Kenny

As we go through life we can be leaders or followers. As a follower you will never get noticed and likely will never make a difference. But life as a follower is safe. Followers don't make waves.

The lion leads a very different life. The lion roars and lets his presence be known. He does things the sheep would never do. The problem with being a lion, however, is there is often a bigger lion who will try to knock you down. But being knocked down once in a while means at least you've made an attempt to rise above the mediocrity of life as a sheep.

Today be a lion.

May 5

"He who is not courageous enough to take risks will accomplish nothing in life."~ Muhammad Ali

Risk does need to be evaluated. Risk and reckless abandon are not the same. To take a risk you must look at the odds and at the potential reward as well as the potential downside. Then go for it. Many times something that one person sees as risky was the only choice for the person who did it. You will never be extraordinary without risk.

You are not capable of failing. Everything you do produces a result. It may not produce the result you had hoped for, but it will produce a result. When you don't get the result you want, learn from that experience and move on.

Today live your life to the fullest, take a risk, take action, and accomplish something.

May 6

"Goliath was the best thing that ever happened to David."
~ Doug Weed

More often than not, the thing that propels a person to greatness is an obstacle he faces. If Mt. Everest were easy to climb, climbing it would be no big deal. If everyone were a millionaire, being a millionaire would not be remarkable.

The obstacles you face keep others from following the same path. The path with few obstacles has many followers and few rewards. The path with the most rewards has the most obstacles, but those obstacles may not be as hard to overcome as they seem. Goliath seemed to be an impossible obstacle. That is why no one would fight him except David. It is possible that anyone could have defeated Goliath, but only one man tried. Have you tried to overcome your obstacles, or have you avoided the obstacles in your path?

Today take one step toward your goal, one step toward overcoming something that is in your way. Then after the first step, take another, and another, and keep moving in the direction you wish to go. You may find that the obstacle was much easier to overcome than you first imagined.

May 7

"Be kind whenever possible. It is always possible."
~ Dalai Lama

This is such a simple idea that we teach it to small children. But as adults we tend to forget it. You know what it means to be kind. And you know if what you are doing is kind or not.

There is a law in the universe that says you get what you give. So if you want people to be kind to you, be kind to them.

This is easy to do with people who are kind. The test comes when you are dealing with people who are unkind. In these situations remember that it is always possible to be kind. And if you give enough kindness, you will get kindness in return. So when the clerk is rude, or the person next to you in line seems grumpy, remember to smile and be kind.

Today be kind to everyone.

May 8

"A smile is the shortest distance between two people."
~ Victor Borge

I try to smile at everyone, even people I pass on the street or in a store. A smile can brighten someone's day. The more joy you spread, the more you will enjoy life.

Today smile at everyone you see - your family, your coworkers, and even strangers. Then enjoy the peace and happiness that comes back to you.

May 9

"There are no mistakes. The events we bring on ourselves, no matter how unpleasant, are necessary in order to learn what we need to learn. Whatever steps we take, they're necessary to reach the places we've chosen to go."~ Richard Bach

Life is meant to be easy, and there are lessons we can learn to make it easy. As we learn these lessons, the world starts to flow around us, and everything just seems to work. When trying times come to you, do not feel sorry for yourself and do not complain. Do two things. Figure out how to resolve the issue, and find the lesson the Universe wants you to learn. When you learn the lesson, that issue will be easier to resolve if it should ever show up again.

Imagine a three year old who throws a temper tantrum every time he is told no. He lies on the floor kicking and screaming until he gets his way. He needs to learn he's not always going to get his way, and his parents need to learn it's okay to say no and not give into his screaming. This situation will keep repeating itself until both parties learn their lesson.

What issues are you having? What are the lessons that can be learned from these issues? They may be hard to see, so keep looking. If you are having health issues, you may need to reduce your stress. If you are having relationship issues, you may need to give more and be more accepting of others. If you are having financial issues, you may need to learn to be grateful for what you have.

Today look for the lessons and remember there are no mistakes.

May 10

"How can I be of the greatest service doing that which I most enjoy doing?"~ Earl Nightingale

What a great question, and what a great way to live your life.

By doing what you enjoy most, you reduce stress and fulfill your life's purpose. You also make it easier to let your true nature, happiness, come out. When you are of service to others, you activate spiritual law. The more you help others and the more you give, the more you will receive.

So by helping the most people, while doing what you love, you allow the life you always imagined to take shape.

Today ask yourself, "How can I be of the greatest service doing that which I most enjoy doing?" When you get an answer, try to move your life in that direction.

May 11

"Success is not the key to happiness. Happiness is the key to success. If you love what you are doing, you will be successful."~ Albert Schweitzer

I think most people have this backwards. Most people are trying so hard to be successful because they think it will bring them happiness. What they do not realize is that they can be happy right now. Happiness is not something you must get. You have it now. You just need to realize that your happiness is inside you. Let it out. Then when you are happy and you love what you are doing, you will be successful.

People are always trying to get more stuff so they can be happy, but when they get new stuff, they find they want even more stuff. Have ambitions and goals, but be happy and thankful for what you have and where you are.

Today be happy now.

May 12

"Don't allow yourself to think of step number two until you've executed step number one."~ Unknown

Do you ever get ahead of yourself? Do you ever lose focus on what you are doing because you are thinking of what you need to do next? It's great to stay focused on the goal and work with the goal in mind, but not at the expense of losing the focus of the moment.

Too often people are not focused on what they are doing. Research has proven that not only is multitasking ineffective, but very few people do it well, regardless of their belief to the contrary. Stop trying to multitask. Break the norm. Do one thing and do it well. Then move on to the next step.

When you focus on the first step, you will finish your task sooner and do a better job. Then you can move on to the next step. You will be more effective, you will get more done, and you will feel more relaxed.

Today focus on what you are doing.

May 13

"You miss 100% of the shots you never take."
~ Wayne Gretzky

And you miss 100% of the opportunities you never act on. Opportunities are all around us, and many are missed due to fear. Fear of failure is a big culprit, but so is fear of success.

If you don't act because of a fear of failing, then you have failed. Not acting on an idea is a sure guarantee that you will never complete the task. There may be opportunities that should be avoided, but many good opportunities are never taken.

Today take a chance, even if you are afraid.

May 14

"Glorify who you are today, do not condemn who you were yesterday, and dream of who you can be tomorrow."
~ Neale Donald Walsch

Live in the moment. This moment is the only time you have the power to do anything. And this is true from moment to moment. Be thankful for your past and know that your future will be great, but live in the moment.

To make your future remarkable, you must take action now that will affect your life tomorrow.

Today live life to the fullest.

May 15

"I choose to be unreasonably happy."~ Brad Yates

The only way to be happy is unreasonably, or without reason. Happiness is not caused by reasons, but it can be blocked by reasons. The happiness inside you is like the light of the sun. The sun's light is always shining, just as your happiness is always inside you. To feel the warmth of the sun, you must remove the blocks between you and the light. You must get out of the house and move out of the shade. Then you can feel the warmth. If you are in a dark room, the sun is still shining, it just isn't apparent to you. When you are in a dark time in your life, your happiness is still there, you are just blocking it from coming out. Remove the blocks and let your happiness flow.

The most common block is desire. When you desire something that isn't in your life, you block happiness because you are focused on something other than the present. Have goals if you wish, but accept that things are the way they are. You may want something better in the future, but instead of focusing on the lack, live as if the wish is already fulfilled. Have the feeling of your desire realized. Transmute your desires into joy and live in the happiness of the moment.

Today choose to be unreasonably happy.

May 16

"Do the thing you fear, and the death of fear is certain."
~ Ralph Waldo Emerson

When there is something you fear and you do that thing, you will likely find that there wasn't anything to be afraid of. The thing we fear the most is the unknown, but when we complete the task, it is no longer unknown.

We often get stuck in fear, and we don't do the things we could or should do. Let your fear go, and live life to its fullest.

Today do something you fear, and let the fear go.

May 17

"The law of flotation was not discovered by studying the sinking of things."~ Thomas Troward

Is there something in your life you would like to accomplish?

Is there something more that you want in your life?

If so, then focus on the accomplishment and having it now, not on the lack of it or it not being done. Eliminate the phrase "I can't" from your vocabulary and replace it with "How can I?" When you ask yourself a question, your brain goes to work on the answer. When you say, "I can't," your brain stops looking for a solution. You can come up with solutions if you just allow yourself the time to figure them out.

Today look at what you want to accomplish. Then ask yourself, "How can I do it?"

May 18

"The way we communicate with others and with ourselves ultimately determines the quality of our lives."
~ Tony Robbins

Just about everything you want or need is owned by someone else. To get those things you must interact with those people. As we go forward in the computer age, some of those dealings can be done with the click of a mouse. Because of this, people are losing their communication skills. As you develop your communication skills, life will be easier. It will be easier to get the things you want, and you will move through life more simply.

The other communication that is important is how you communicate with yourself. When your self-talk is negative, turn it around. When you notice a negative thought, replace it immediately with a positive thought. When you catch yourself thinking, "I don't have enough," change your thought to, "I am abundant, and I live in an abundant world." Repeat the positive affirmation ten times to remove the negative thought. If you do this repeatedly, you will find your thoughts are mostly positive.

Today practice communicating. Listen to the person you are with and listen to your own thoughts.

May 19

"Friendship is not something you learn in school. But if you haven't learned the meaning of friendship, you really haven't learned anything."~ Muhammad Ali

I think friendship can be something you learn in school, but it isn't in any of the textbooks. I think school is where you learn how to be a friend and what you expect of your friends. And I think this lesson is more important than memorizing dates or solving equations.

Spend time every day for the next month reconnecting with old friends or making the connection with your current friends stronger. Take a little bit of time every day to improve your connection with a friend. Then make sure you nurture your friendships.

You may have learned that the best way to be a friend is to be the person that you would like to be friends with. But this doesn't always work. When you ask your friends what they want from a friend, it may be different than what you want. So as a friend, make sure you're meeting the needs of your friends. And to me that's what a good friend is.

Today be a good friend.

May 20

"Happiness is a journey, not a destination; happiness is to be found along the way not at the end of the road, for then the journey is over and it's too late. The time for happiness is today not tomorrow."~ Paul H. Dunn

Do you believe that you need something or someone to be happy?

Are you trying to get a new car, a new house, or a new spouse so you can be happy?

Happiness is not in any of those things. Happiness is inside of you. When you get the new car, you decide to be happy, but the happiness comes from you. If you don't believe me think about this.

Imagine you just got home and you find a note from someone you love very much that says, "My uncle sent me a huge check so I decided to get you the car of your dreams, and I am out getting it right now. I am paying cash for it so it will be all yours. Be home soon. Love,..."

Would you be excited and happy? You would in spite of the fact that you haven't gotten to drive the car, sit in the car, or even see the car yet. You are happy not because of the car but because you decided to be happy. Every day people are happy to get "new" used cars that other people were happy to get rid of. The happiness is not in the car. It is in you. And you can substitute anything in this world for car and it is still true.

Stop searching for something to make you happy and decide to be happy now. Release what is keeping you from the happiness you want. When you think that the new car will make you happy, the source of the unhappiness is not having the car. You believe you can't be happy until you get the car. Change that belief and be happy now. Stop wanting the world to be different than it is, and your happiness will flow.

Today decide to be happy.

May 21

"You see people not as they are but as you are."
~ Anthony deMello

Your world is a reflection of you. The people in your life are treating you exactly how you have taught them to treat you. For some this is hard to accept, but the role of the victim does not serve you. When you play the victim, you give away the power to control your life.

Stop playing the victim. Start looking at yourself and the people around you in a new way. Learn to let the happiness and love inside you come forth, and see the people in your life as the loving expressions of God that they truly are. Remember that everyone is motivated by what he or she wants. The person who helps and the person who hurts are both fulfilling a selfish desire.

When you can understand why you do what you do, it will be easier to understand why you see others as you do. Change the way you see yourself, and the way you see the people around you will change.

Today see the good in everyone, especially yourself.

May 22

"The Holy Spirit knows what your rent is."
~ Marianne Williamson

Sometimes we forget this. The source of your income is not your job or your customers. Everything comes from The Divine - everything. The Divine creates everything. When you are in line with The Divine and your divine purpose, then abundance can flow to you. Your employer may write the check, but be sure that the source is The Holy Spirit.

I have seen this many times in my life. When I let go and release my fear or worry, what I need comes to me. This can be money, or people, or even situations. Whatever I need is there if I just let go and follow inspiration. So let go and know that whatever you need is there for you if you just allow it to come to you.

Today turn your problems over to The Divine. Let go and let God.

May 23

"The first step to getting the things you want out of life is this: Decide what you want."~ Ben Stein

Decide what you want and be specific. We often change what we want from minute to minute. If you don't have a specific goal, how will you ever get there? And if you do get there, how will you know?

When you get in your car, 99% of the time you know where you are going and how you are going to get there, and usually you arrive at your destination. But have you ever started daydreaming about something and your internal auto pilot drove you to the wrong place? It has happened to all of us. We loose focus on our destination and miss our goal.

The same is true in life. You need to decide where you want to go and then focus on that goal until you arrive there. When you take on a task, ask yourself if it is helping you move toward your goal or moving you away from your goal.

Today decide where you want to go with your life and move in that direction.

May 24

"There is no use in using a logical argument against an illogical point of view."~ Anne Rose

From time to time you will meet people with a different point of view than yours. If you are both open to discussion, this can be a great opportunity to expand your point of view. Use these opportunities to grow and learn.

However, sometimes you will meet people who have a point of view that is not supported by logic. Arguing with them is like trying to argue with a child or someone who has dementia or Alzheimer's. It is fruitless, pointless, and a waste of time. It's best to just let them think what they want without disagreeing with them. People with phobias and people with fanatical beliefs often fall into this category.

If you meet someone who seems to be rational in most aspects of his life but has a belief that is completely illogical, your first thought may be to try to convince him otherwise. Don't waste your time. Your logic will be lost on him.

Today decide to be happy rather than right.

May 25

In this world you must be oh so smart or oh so pleasant. Well, for years I was smart. I recommend pleasant. You may quote me."~ Elwood P. Dowd from the movie *Harvey*

Being pleasant and nice are so much fun. You are choosing your mood. If you choose to be happy, then a pleasant disposition comes naturally. When you decide to be happy and pleasant all of the time, you will find that fewer things upset you. By choosing to be pleasant, the people you have seen as problems may just become friends.

Today be the bright spot in the life of everyone you meet.

May 26

A good laugh is sunshine in a house."
~ William Makepeace Thackeray

How often do you laugh?

Maybe more important is how often do you laugh at yourself?

There are times when a situation dictates being serious, but there are lots of times when laughter will help diffuse a tense situation. Look for things that are funny, try to find the humor all around you, and when you see it, laugh. Then look for the humor in what you do, and laugh at yourself.

When you laugh, you break down barriers. When you laugh at yourself, if change is needed, it becomes easier. When you laugh at yourself, you also take yourself less seriously, and doing that is usually a great idea. When you laugh, it brightens everyone around you.

Today laugh.

May 27

"Love is an element which though physically unseen is as real as air or water. It is an acting, living, moving force... it moves in waves and currents like those of the ocean."
~ Prentice Mulford

Love is real. I know it cannot be measured by a machine in a lab, but it is just as real as something that can be. In fact, it is even more real. Love is God expressing himself through you.

When you give love, you are giving the experience of God, and nothing is more real or true than God.

As the waves of love ebb and flow, remember that it is not God's love that is changing, but rather your awareness of your connection with God. God's love is never ending and never changing, and your connection with God is also just as strong and enduring. When you don't feel love, it is because you are not aware of your connection with God.

There are many things in this world that we are not aware of. Right now you are flying around the Sun at over 60,000 mph. Just because you don't feel the motion does not mean it is not happening. The same is true with love. Just because you are not feeling the love of God does not mean it isn't there. Open your heart to feel the love that God is giving you in every moment. Then share that love with everyone you meet.

Today open your heart to love.

May 28

"It is amazing what you can accomplish if you do not care who gets the credit." ~ Harry Truman

When you are concerned about who gets the credit, two things happen. First, if you want all the credit for yourself, you may be less likely to implement or even welcome other people's ideas. And second, you may be less likely to take risks since wanting all the credit also means you would have to accept all the blame if your idea or plan fails.

Do what is best for the group as a whole. Let your ego take a backseat. Go into a project with the idea that you will give away all the credit or take all the blame. When you have that mind set, you are much more likely to do something great.

Today give the credit to someone else and take the blame for something.

May 29

"The world is full of abundance and opportunity, but far too many people come to the fountain of life with a sieve instead of a tank car... a teaspoon instead of a steam shovel. They expect little and as a result they get little."~ Ben Sweetland

Are you experiencing all of the abundance the world has to offer?

What are you expecting? Do you expect abundance or lack?

It is hard to expect something different than the reality you are currently experiencing, but this is the key. Focus on the abundance. Focus on the good. Look at nature. In nature God produces in abundance. That same abundance can be experienced in your life. Be open to receive the abundance and focus on the good. Then know that the good is larger than you could ever imagine. Think big, dream big, and expect great things.

Repeat these sentences (several times if you wish):

I am abundant.
I only see the good in the world.
I am grateful for all that I have.
All that I could ever need or want is here for me.
I know great things are coming into my life.

Today live in abundance.

May 30

"People are anxious to improve their circumstances but unwilling to improve themselves. Therefore they remain forever bound."~ James Allen

If bookstores replaced their self-help sections with how -to-fix-other-people sections, they would probably sell more books. But we can't change other people. We can only change ourselves. Changing your habits and your way of thinking is not always easy, but it is the only way to change your situation.

Is there anything about yourself that you would like to change? Would you like to be more abundant? More caring? More patient? More dedicated to work or family? Work on changing just one thing until that part of your life is where you want it to be, then work on something else. By focusing on one area at a time, you will see more results.

Today do something to improve yourself.

May 31

"How people treat you is their karma; how you react is yours."
~ Wayne Dyer

As you go through life, there will be people who do things you don't like. You can't always choose what happens to you, but you can always choose how you react.

If you lose your job, you could blame your employer and feel sorry for yourself, or you could view it as an opportunity to find a better job. One option keeps you stuck in self pity, while the other option opens up a new world. When a waitress is rude, you can be rude back, or you can rise above that and say something nice to brighten her day. When you rise above, you are expressing your true loving self and brightening the world.

You can react to anything in a positive way. You can view any event as an opportunity, and you can be the light of the world. Respond to everything and everyone with love and gratitude.

Today be loving.

June 1

"We do not know one millionth of one percent about anything."~ Thomas Edison

Thomas Edison was one of the most brilliant people who ever lived. He earned over one thousand patents, more than any other person in U.S. history. So one of the smartest men in history believed we know just a tiny fraction of what there is to know, and he was right.

Information is available to us today at a rate faster than ever before, with no end in sight. When we realize how little we know, it opens up a world of possibilities. We may discover that something we once thought to be impossible is now a possibility.

Today think about what you could do if the impossible were an option.

June 2

"The standard of success in life isn't the things. It isn't the money or the stuff. It is absolutely the amount of joy you feel."~ Ester and Jerry Hicks

Money is neutral, not good and not bad. If you spend all of your time worried about money, you might feel miserable. On the other hand, if you enjoy the money you have and are thankful for every penny, money can bring you great joy. So if you want to be happy, change your attitude toward stuff. Be grateful for all of your stuff and enjoy life.

Today adopt an attitude of gratitude. Be thankful for all that you have - money, possessions, health, relationships, and opportunities.

June 3

"Peace is inevitable for those who offer peace."
~ *A Course in Miracles*

The easiest way to get something is to give it. I know it sounds counterintuitive, but it is true. If you want love, give love. If you want happiness, give happiness. If you want peace, give peace.

When you see people around you in conflict, fear, or anger, give them peace. Be a calming force in their lives. It isn't necessary to agree or disagree with their opinions. Just calmly listen and think thoughts of peace and resolution. Your calm energy will be enough, and as a result you will be more at peace.

Today allow the peace of the world to start with you.

June 4

"Happiness depends upon ourselves."~ Aristotle

You choose if you are happy or not. No one can choose for you, and no one can force you to be upset if you choose to be happy.

To test this think about someone with whom you are mad. That person did or said something that upset you, right? If that is true, then you have allowed that person to control how you feel, and since you have given him that power, does he also get to decide when you will stop feeling mad? Of course not because in truth he has absolutely no power over your emotions. But because he did or said something that you didn't like, you chose to get mad and then you chose to blame him for the way you felt. The truth is only *you* can choose how you feel at any given moment. You are 100% responsible for the way you feel.

The only person who has been there every time you were mad is you. So you are the one who controls if you are happy or not. When you decide that you are going to be happy no matter what happens, then you have control of your life.

Today choose to be happy.

June 5

"True love is rooted in acceptance, grows in gratitude, and blooms in happiness."~ Mark Rose

For most people love is an exchange of services. You do this for me, and I will do that for you, but if you break any of my rules, I will take my love away. This works for contracts and business but not for love.

To truly love people, first you must accept them exactly as they are. If you want them to change, you are not loving them.

Second, be thankful for them and all they do. When you accept them, it is easy to be grateful for them. The attitude of gratitude will replace the feelings of fear, anger, or envy and allow your love to grow.

Finally, be happy. This will come naturally. Since you have removed all of the negative emotions, your love will bloom.

Give love and don't ask for or expect anything in return.

Today love unconditionally.

June 6

"Unless you walk out into the unknown, the odds of making a profound difference in your life are pretty low."
~ Tom Peters

If you keep doing what you've always done, you will keep getting what you've always got. Routine is fine, and if you are happy with where you are in your life, then keep doing the same stuff. However, if you want your life to change, then you need to change what you do. You must do the unknown. You can do things that no one has ever done, or you can mold your life after the life of someone you respect and admire. Either way choose what you want and decide how to get where you want to go.

The unknown doesn't need to be scary. It is just unknown. Stop living through habit and embrace the unknown.

Today do something new.

June 7

"If you must doubt something, doubt your limits."
~ Price Pritchett

The one thing that is holding you back from greatness more than anything else is you. We all have limiting beliefs. The more successful a person is, the fewer limiting beliefs he has. You were born to be great. Allow your greatness to come through by changing what you think is possible.

Look at one limiting belief. Really examine it. See if that belief could be false. Just look for the possibility. When you find the possibility, change the belief to a belief that will not hold you back. Change I can't to how can I. Let go of your limiting beliefs, and open up to unlimited possibilities.

Today try something new.

June 8

"Be thankful for what you have; you'll end up having more. If you concentrate on what you don't have, you will never, ever have enough."~ Oprah Winfrey

What do you focus on? Where is your attention going? Are you experiencing lack? Are you focused on not having enough? If so, change your focus. Be thankful for the blessings that are in your life right now. When you start to focus on your blessings, you may be surprised at how many there are.

When you're focusing on lack, complaining about what you don't have, or whining about what you want, you're in a very negative state of mind. To reverse this, start being grateful and thankful for all the blessings you have. Doing this will put you in a positive state of mind. Focus on the good, focus on the abundance, and focus on all the wonderful things in your life. Then, and only then, will you start to acquire more of the things you want.

Today be thankful and focus on the good.

June 9

"The ability to be in the present moment is a major component of mental wellness."~ Abraham Maslow

The most common mental illness in this country today is stress, and stress can be described as fear or regret. People who are stressed are worried about an event that may or may not happen or upset about an event that has already happened. If you can get away from that and focus on the present moment, there is no stress.

If you are experiencing stress in this moment, then you are not experiencing this moment. You are thinking about the future or the past. Get in this moment and enjoy it or hate it, but experience it. Then experience the next moment.

Today live in this moment.

June 10
"Be good at letting go."~ Marsha Sinetar

Often our problems are a result of not letting go. When we cling to the past, we are avoiding the present. Focusing on the past keeps you from doing anything right now to improve your future. There is no power in the past. The only power you have is now. Now is the only time that exists. Spend your time right now focused on right now and let go of your past.

If you were hurt by someone, forgive him and move on. The decision to have that person as a part of your life is a decision you can make now. Forgive him and let go of any negative emotions, and then decide if you want to spend time with him or not. You can love him and accept who he is, but that doesn't mean you need him in your life.

Today forgive and let go.

June 11

"It's fun to be on the edge. I think you do your best work when you take chances, when you're not safe, when you're not in the middle of the road, at least for me, anyway."
~ Danny DeVito

Don't be afraid of the edge. The middle isn't safe. It just seems that way. When you live your life in the middle, you have zero chance of being great. When you live your life at the edge, you have more fun, and you can be amazing.

Take chances. Do things that are fun, exciting, and different. Live life to the fullest.

Today take a chance and push yourself further than you normally would.

June 12

"The less secure a man is, the more likely he is to have extreme prejudice."~ Clint Eastwood

When a person has self-confidence, he is less concerned with what other people are doing. When I am confident in my beliefs, whether you agree or disagree with me doesn't matter to me. When a person spends his time trying to convince others to agree with him, he is often trying to convince himself. When a person knows that what he believes is right for him and is in line with the Truth, then he is much more willing to listen to the opinions of other people.

People who do not feel secure in their own beliefs are much more likely to judge the beliefs of others as wrong. These judgements often involve the beliefs of people of different races, nationalities, religions, or political affiliations. Insecure people feel threatened by anyone or anything that is different than they are. Pre-judging the beliefs of others as wrong or bad is simply a means of reinforcing their own beliefs as correct, thereby keeping the world around them small and safe.

When you are open to the ideas and thoughts of other people, you are open to grow. Allow other people to think what they want without judging them. Be open to ideas that contradict your beliefs. You don't need to change your beliefs. Just listen and be willing to entertain new ideas.

Today be secure in your ideas but be open to new ones too.

June 13

"Act boldly and unseen forces will come to your aid."~Dorothea Brande

Bold actions create big results. So if you are going to be taking action anyway, why not make it a bold action? Sometimes a bold action takes more skill, but not always. Sometimes it just takes more guts.

If you can call a big client or a small client, call the big one. If you can choose between a little idea and a grand idea, choose the grand one. Instead of helping one person, help one hundred people.

When you think big and take bold action, the world will help you. To be great you need to do things that other people have not done. This is being bold. And the universe likes greatness. When you do a great deed with great love, the universe will set in motion the people and resources you need to complete the project. When you do small things, you are on your own.

Today think big, take big action, and be bold.

June 14

"If it ain't fun, don't do it!"~ Jack Canfield

This is one of my favorite quotes and truly words to live by. I have fun all of the time. I spend my days doing things I enjoy.

When a situation arises that I don't enjoy, I have two choices. I either make it fun or stop doing it.

There are people I don't spend time with because they seem to fight life rather than enjoy it. That's their choice. I don't judge them. They are simply in a different place than I am, so I minimize my time around them.

I try to make everything I do fun. There are many ways to do this, and what works for me may not work for you.

Today have fun, play, and act like a kid. Your soul will appreciate it.

June 15

"Once you experience forgiveness, your outer world changes."
~ Joe Vitale

Forgiveness is one of the greatest gifts you can give yourself. Forgiving is not for the benefit of anyone except you. When you hold a grudge or harbor a resentment, the negative feelings are in you, not anyone else. The anger, the hatred, the bitterness, all that negativity, is part of you. When you forgive, all of those bad feelings are released from you, not the person you forgive. You are the one who receives all of the benefits of forgiving.

When you forgive, a weight is lifted from you. This allows you to live a freer life. By releasing the negative energy, your eyes open to a new world, a world that always existed but was hidden from view.

Today forgive just one person. Then forgive yourself for judging that person.

June 16

"Just because the party's over doesn't mean it wasn't a good party."~ Mike Lowe

The world and our lives are constantly changing. Just like the seasons change from winter to spring, so must our lives change.

For someone who lost a job, this may seem hard, but know that opportunity is waiting for you if you are open to see it. Have the attitude of gratitude for the new opportunity. Be thankful knowing that it will arrive at just the right moment.

Where matters of the heart are concerned, remember that just because a relationship ends or is changing, it doesn't mean it wasn't good while it lasted. Remember the good times, remember what the other person taught you, and be grateful that you were both able to grow. Take the lessons from your last relationship and apply them to your next relationship. Take the time to learn who you are and who you are growing into. Life is always changing. Accept the change, embrace it, and take the lessons from the past with you as you move forward.

The only constant is change. Your choices are to embrace it or fight it. If you choose to fight, the time will likely come when you accept the change anyway, so save yourself the time and aggravation and accept the change now.

Today be grateful for your past. It made you who you are. Now you can accept the changes in your life and start looking for the opportunities.

June 17

"Choosing to be positive and having a grateful attitude is going to determine how you're going to live your life."
~ Joel Osteen

You get to choose how you are going to live your life. You can be grateful, or you can be a victim. The problem with being a victim is that for your life to get better, whatever situation you feel is causing you to feel victimized must change. So as a victim you are helpless.

When you decide to take control of your life and see the blessings in every event, you can create your life to be whatever you want. And because you are looking for the blessings, they will be easier to see.

Today decide how your life will be instead of leaving it up to chance.

June 18

"Life consists not in holding good cards but in playing those you hold well."~ Josh Billings

Doyle Brunson proved this. He won two World Series of Poker titles with the worst possible hands. Wayne Dyer proved this after being born in an unstable home. The list of notable people who started with nothing and went on to be highly successful is too long to list here. Just know that to get to where you want to be, you must start where you are.

Are you looking at what you don't have, or are you focusing on where you want to be? Look at everything you have in your life that is truly valuable - your health, your brain, your will, your friends, your family. All of these most valuable things are available to you now. You have wealth beyond belief. What are you going to do with it?

Today focus on doing the most you can with what you have.

June 19

"Almost any decision is better than no decision at all."
~ Brian Tracy

Some people suffer from paralysis through over analysis. Some people have never learned how to make decisions, while others are just afraid to make decisions. Whatever the reason, not making decisions isn't productive or effective. When you don't make a decision, the decision will be made for you. Either someone else will decide for you, or your inaction will become your decision.

Imagine you are thinking about buying a particular used car you saw advertised. If you think about the decision too long, the car may be sold to someone else. Or imagine a friend asking you where you want to eat, but you can't decide. Your indecision could result in your having to eat in a restaurant you don't like. When you don't take action, someone else will.

To get better at decision making, just start making choices. Choose where you want to eat, and when you get to the restaurant, look at the menu and choose something. Don't hem and haw and wait to see what everyone else is getting before you decide. Whenever someone asks you something, have an opinion, make a choice, make a decision. When you start deciding on the little things, it makes the big decisions easier.

Today make a decision.

June 20

"Complete possession is proved only by giving. All you are unable to give possesses you."~ Andre Gide

When you become so attached to something that you can't give it away, that thing then controls your life, or at least part of your life. The thing can be a possession, a person, a job, or even an idea.

When you are able to let these things go, then you have freedom. Often when I tell people this, the first question they ask is about their spouse. And I think this is one of the hardest but most important lessons to learn. When you truly love your spouse, and you care for his or her well being and happiness, why would you want him or her to be unhappy? If your spouse's choice is to be happy without you rather than unhappy with you, and you expect him or her to remain unhappy, then you are being selfish. I believe in giving your all to make a marriage work and sticking with your partner through challenging times, but if the relationship ends, allow the other person to be happy, and you will be happier too.

Today give up the need for one thing. Keep it in your life, but know that you would still be just fine without it.

June 21

"Give a man a fish and you feed him for a day. Teach a man to fish and you feed him for a lifetime."~ Lao Tzu

Most of us have hard this before and would agree that it is true. But do we apply it in our lives? Teaching someone how to do something is usually more difficult than just doing it ourselves.

In the world of business, the best leaders seem to do nothing, yet are very respected. These leaders have taught the people they lead how to do what needs to be done. The result is freedom of time for the leader and a sense of accomplishment for the worker. When we can help others to feel good about themselves, we gain respect.

Children are born depending on their parents and often continue to rely on them well into adulthood. However, the great parents are the ones who can teach their children how to live independently.

Many times we are looking for the quick solution, and doing the task is easier than teaching the task, but in doing that there is little gain for either party. When we teach someone how to do something, their dependence on us lessens, and that may be the very reason we don't want to teach them. We are afraid that if we teach them too much, we will not be needed, when actually the opposite is true. As we teach, we often gain respect, and a leader, friend, or parent who is respected is more valuable than a leader who is needed for a particular skill.

Today teach something and everyone involved will have the opportunity to grow.

June 22

"I can't feel bad enough to put myself in a more positive place."~ Brad Yates

This seems obvious, I know. But have you ever had an event in your life that you reacted to with negative emotions? The only way to get over your negative reaction is to "re-act" in a positive way. When you are in a positive place, negative events are less common.

When an event causes a negative reaction, switch to feeling good as soon as possible. Start to tell yourself you feel good even if you don't. Tell yourself you are happy even if you are not. Telling yourself to feel good will trigger those feelings, and when you feel good, life is better.

Today feel good no matter what happens.

June 23

"It's a great day. Now, go make it that way."
~ Robert G. Allen

Your day is completely under your control. You may not have control over the events of your day, but you can control how you react to those events.

Today will be a great day if you decide to make it that way.

June 24

"If a man insisted always on being serious, and never allowed himself a bit of fun and relaxation, he would go mad or become unstable without knowing it."~ Herodotus

Have you ever met people who are serious all the time? They are focused on getting work done, or being proper, or not offending anyone. These kinds of people are actually focused on themselves. They tend to get caught up in their own importance. They start to think that everything they do is going to change the world. These are not the type of people you want to spend time with.

When we think about the people we enjoy spending time with, they are usually more relaxed, funnier, and sometimes they say things that aren't proper. These people do not take themselves too seriously. They are not afraid to laugh at themselves.

Think about yourself. Are you fun? Can you laugh at yourself? Can you step away from the serious things in your life? Now is the time to look at yourself and decide if you want more fun and relaxation in your life. If so, you can change and be the person you want to be.

Today relax, have fun, and laugh at yourself.

June 25

"There is no such thing as failure. There are only results."
~ Tony Robbins

Failure is just a perception. When people say they failed, what they really mean is that they didn't get the result they had hoped for. People who become hugely successful all learn this lesson. They take risks and learn from the results. They release the fear of failing because they know that whatever they do will give them a result.

When you can change your idea of failure, possibilities open up. To really understand this, look at your past and think of a time you think you failed. Did your actions produce a result? If they did, you succeeded. If you want different results, then you need to change your actions. Now that you know this, you can change your actions next time.

Today eliminate failure from your vocabulary and examine your actions. Are they leading to the results you desire?

June 26

"I like thinking big. If you're going to be thinking anything, you might as well think big."~ Donald Trump

The Romans were great at thinking big. In the year 80 A.D., the Colosseum, a 50,000 seat arena with a retractable roof, was finished. It took almost 1900 years before another stadium that size was built. If the Romans had built the Smalliseum, do you think anyone would go visit it today?

When you think small, you are not just limiting yourself, you are limiting the world. You are here to do great magnificent things. Stop thinking small and step into your greatness. Then if your first great thing does not succeed, try something else great. When you think of the first Ford, you think Model T, but there were nineteen models or prototypes, models A-S, built in the five years before the Model T. Then when the Model T was retired, Ford started fresh again with the Model A because the Model A was not an improved Model T but a reinvention of the car.

When your success is big enough, your failures will be forgotten. When you think of TV producer, Mark Burnett, what show do you think of? *Survivor? The Apprentice?* or *Commando Nanny?*

Today think big.

June 27

"Most of the successful people I've known are the ones who do more listening than talking."~ Bernard M. Baruch

There is a reason we have two ears and one mouth. We should listen twice as much as we talk. The people we like the most are the people who are genuinely interested in us and listen to us.

The easiest way to show that you are interested in someone is to listen to him. Care about what he is saying and focus on him. If you do this one simple thing, people will like and respect you more.

When you listen, you are gaining knowledge and insight. This will help you in all of your relationships. But you need to be really interested. If you fake it, people will see through the insincerity.

Today listen to the people you talk to and care about what they are saying.

June 28

"It is not what we take up, but what we give up, that makes us rich."~ Henry Ward Beecher

The focus in society today is on getting more stuff, but the more stuff you have the less freedom you have. The more you value a thing, the more likely it is to tie you down. Imagine if you owned a $500,000 Ferrari. Would you be scared to leave it parked on the street or in a mall parking lot? Would you want to put 15,000 miles a year on it? Would you drive it in the rain and snow? Or, would you have another car for daily use and only drive the Ferrari on special occasions? You might be so worried about your car that you would feel stressed every time you drove it. You may be giving up your freedom and your peace of mind just to own that car. The same principal applies to everything in your life.

When you give up the things in your life, you get your life back. The less stuff you have, the more freedom you have. You get to choose. You may decide to give up some of your freedom for a child, a spouse, or a pet, but make sure that you are making that decision fully aware of what you are getting and what you are giving up. How you decide is up to you. And if you decide to own the Ferrari, just make sure the Ferrari does not own you.

Today let go of something in your life.

June 29

"Complaining is like bad breath, you notice it when it comes out of somebody else's mouth, but not your own."
~ Will Bowen

Most people complain from time to time, but some people complain all of the time. As much as you would like to point this out to them, the best thing to do is just notice your own complaining.

When you complain, you block the good from flowing in your life. You can restart this flow by being aware of what you say and by refusing to say anything that even remotely seems like a complaint. But you cannot stop your complaining until you are aware of it.

When you catch yourself complaining, replace the complaint with a positive thought. When you stop complaining, your friends and family will see the change, and then you can share what you did.

Today be aware of your thoughts and words.

June 30

"Everything you want and you don't have, you get from other people."~ Marshall Sylver

This is an important fact to know. As our world becomes more electronic, some people are losing the skills needed to interact with each other. I can think of many things I have bought without ever talking to a real person. The farther we go down this path, the more difficult it is going to be, especially for young people, to learn how to interact with other people.

Take the time to examine your relationships and your ability to interact with others. Then teach your children the importance of one on one communication. Earlier generations learned this skill because there was no other option. We could very easily raise a society of poor communicators but great texters. Don't let this happen. Force your children and yourself to refine your ability to talk to people face to face.

Practice your communication skills and learn how to say the things you are afraid to voice. Then teach these skills to your children. People learn by example, so be the example of a great communicator.

Today really talk to people.

July 1

"If you follow the herd, you end up stepping in crap."
~ Wayne Dyer

No one ever achieved anything great by doing what everyone else was doing, exactly like everyone else was doing it. Greatness can only come from being different. Many people view being different as risky, and it is true that when you do things differently, there is a chance of failing. But I think the greater risk is in never trying.

When you do things just like everyone else, you are almost guaranteed to be mediocre. If you want to be mediocre, then go for it. But if you want to be extraordinary, then do something different. Personally, I would rather risk failure than be guaranteed mediocrity.

Today be different.

July 2

"The thing is, we have to let go of all blame, all attacking, all judging, to free our inner selves to attract what we say we want. Until we do, we are hamsters in a cage chasing our own tails and wondering why we aren't getting the results we seek."~ Joe Vitale

Blaming is easy, and it's such a great way to divert responsibility from ourselves. All of us have blamed someone for something. We have all judged other people. And we have all attacked another, if not physically then verbally. It is also likely that we will all do these things again.

When we blame, what we are saying is, "It isn't my fault." The problem with this is it's not solution oriented. When we can accept just some or all of the responsibility, then we can move toward a solution. Even if you didn't create the problem, saying, "I am sorry," will get you further then, "It isn't my fault. He did it!"

Judgement is just how we view the world and the people in it. Two people may see the same event or person in a very different light. Abraham Lincoln was both a hero and a villain. It just depended on your opinion and where you lived. Instead of judging, try to look at the world from a neutral point of view.

We all agree that physically hurting another person is not a good thing to do. But how often do we hurt others with our words? People often use guilt, shame, and anger to inflict pain without ever clenching a fist. Think about what you say and how you say it. Be kind to the people you care about as well as to strangers.

Today stop chasing your tail. Get off the wheel of negative thinking and emotions and free yourself.

July 3
"To observe without evaluating is the highest form of intelligence."~ Jiddu Krishnamurti

When we evaluate, we label and judge from our limited point of view. When we define something, we limit it to that definition.

Look at a tree. Look at the leaves, the branches, the bark. As you look, can one word truly describe what you are seeing? How about a hundred words, or a thousand words? Now think of all of the other trees you have seen. Are they all the same? The essence of a tree cannot be contained in a word.

Now think of yourself. How many words would it take to fully describe you and your personality? Have you ever fallen into the trap of labeling and evaluating others or yourself with just a few words? He's lazy. She's selfish. I'm a procrastinator.

See the world in a new way. Look at everything with fresh eyes and without judgement. You will be amazed at what you are able to see.

Today remove the labels. Try to view the world as fresh and new. Observe the world without judging.

July 4

"All seasons are beautiful for the person who carries happiness within."~ Horace Friess

Horace Friess wasn't talking about summer or winter, but rather the seasons of our lives. A season in your life can be a period of growth, a period of rest, a beginning, an end, a period of excitement, or a period of peace. All of these seasons can be beautiful. And if you have happiness within you, they will be.

Today look at this season in your life, and identify where you are. Then look for the beauty.

July 5

"Always forgive your enemies - nothing annoys them so much."~ Oscar Wilde

Forgiving your enemies is the only way to turn them into friends. What did they do that made them enemies in the first place? Start there with your forgiveness. Forgive completely, and learn to love the people you once thought of as enemies.

We are all children of the same God, and God is in all of us. When you see that, you are wise. When you know that, you are forgiving. When you live that, you are enlightened.

Make everyone your friend. See God in every person you speak to.

Today forgive your enemies.

July 6

"Man cannot discover new oceans unless he has the courage to lose sight of the shore."~ Andre Gide

Imagine a cruise ship with thousands of people on board. They leave the harbor headed for new adventures. Then two miles out to sea they turn around and go back to the same dock. Do you think this would be a popular cruise? No. Travelers want to explore new lands and see new things. We know that most cruise ships are safe, so we have no problem leaving the shore, but what about your life?

Are you living your life on the dock, not wanting to take any risks? Open yourself up to new horizons. Do something new and adventurous. Sail into uncharted waters. If you don't, the scenery of your life will never change.

Today have the courage to do something new.

July 7

"Reality is merely an illusion, albeit a very persistent one."
~ Albert Einstein

Quantum physics has a theory that says, " The observing of an event alters the event." Another fact that was known to Einstein is that atoms are mostly empty space. The things in this world we see as solid are actually over 99% empty space. Einstein knew about these facts and concluded that the world we see is only in our minds.

The world is an illusion. This leads us to the question, if the world is only in our minds, can we change our world with our thoughts? The simple answer is yes. You create your world with your thoughts.

Ask yourself if you are creating the world you wish to create? Then remember that the only things you can change are your thoughts. When the world changes, it is reacting to the change in you. Think thoughts of the world you wish to live in and that world will be yours. And if a negative thought comes up, gently dismiss it and replace it with ten positive thoughts.

Today choose your thoughts carefully.

July 8

"Muddy water, let stand, becomes clear."~ Lao Tzu

I have thought about this quote for a of couple weeks. There is more wisdom here than is first obvious. I think this principle can be applied to most every aspect of your life.

There are times when life seems muddy or clouded, times when the next course of action is unclear or when you are so far in your rut that no other course seems possible. You could be so overwhelmed by all of the things you need to do that nothing gets done.

When you are in a situation like this, taking action seems like the thing to do, and it can be, but first stop. Stop and take some time for things to settle. Take time to gain a new perspective. It could be for a minute, ten minutes, an hour, or longer. Just take time to stop and breathe. You can call this meditation, prayer, relaxing, or centering yourself. The label is unimportant.

Sit quietly and clear your mind. Think about something you love. Focus on something other than the mud in your life. The longer you do this, the clearer everything will become.

Do this every day, several times a day. The more you are still, the clearer your life will become. We are in the age of information overload. Let go of the information and connect with inspiration.

Today be still, if only for a little while. I know this one idea can change your life.

July 9

"It is very easy to forgive others their mistakes; it takes more grit and gumption to forgive them for having witnessed your own."~ Jessamyn West

We all have made mistakes, and we all will continue to make mistakes. We know that about ourselves, but we forget that about others. When someone else sees our mistakes, this can be devastating to our ego. People often spend much time and effort trying to hide their faults and protect their ego. When our faults are seen by others, we need to forgive ourselves and forgive the others for their judgement of us.

When you judge others, you are protecting your ego. Let go of the need to judge, and forgive the people who judge you. Release your ego and the ego's need to be separate from everything. We are connected.

Today let go and forgive.

July 10

"How long you live is irrelevant. It is the quality of life that matters."~ Stuart Wilde

You don't know when you will leave this earth, so make every moment of your life magnificent. Then you will have an amazing life.

Often people live for the future. They can't wait until the weekend, or they are waiting for vacation. The problem is when you are waiting for the future, you miss the present, and the present is where the fun is. The present is where life happens. The present is all that matters. So think about the future if you want to, but focus on the now. Make the most of where you are and what you are doing right now. Then when you look back you will see you have lived an amazing life.

Today focus on the quality of your life not the quantity.

July 11

"If you obey all the rules you miss all the fun."
~ Katherine Hepburn

Rules can have their place, but they can also be very limiting. Be respectful of others, be kind, be loving, but don't follow all the rules.

Most rules say do it like this because we have always done it like this. Most rules say act a certain way because it is considered proper. Most rules say don't color outside of the lines, and don't get out of this box.

No one ever did anything extraordinary by following all the rules.

Today have fun, break some rules, and be extraordinary.

July 12
"Do or do not, there is no try."~Yoda

What I believe Yoda and George Lucas in *Star Wars* were going for is a mindset or an attitude. If you believe you will accomplish a task, then you will keep working until you do. If you say, "I am going to run a marathon," then you have eliminated all doubt in doing so. You eliminate the possibility of failure. If you say, "I am going to *try* to run a marathon," then the possibility of not running twenty-six miles comes into play. You may end up saying, "I tried to run a marathon but only made it to the front porch, but I tried."

Trying to do something is not actually doing it. You tried to get out of bed this morning but you are still in bed. You tried to fix the car, but it's still broken. However, if you got out of bed and fixed the car, you are in a very different place.

When you have a task to complete, set in your mind the belief that you will complete the task. Eliminate any possibility of failure. Know with all of your heart that you will finish the task. Don't try to do it, be like Nike and just do it.

Today believe you can do it.

July 13
"Don't be afraid to give up the good to go for the great."
~ John D. Rockefeller

Are you stuck in good? Good is good, but great is better. People fear the unknown more than anything else, but it is only when they are willing to leave their comfort zone and face their fear of the unknown that they can arrive at greatness.

For some people the idea of leaving a job or changing careers is scary. For many people a bad relationship is better than no relationship. Let go of these fears. Good enough is not good enough. Stop doing what you have always done and start doing something new. Go for the greatness.

It may not be easy, and your life may change in ways that you didn't expect, but embrace those changes and welcome the greatness into your life.

Today be great.

July 14

"Stress is an inappropriate fight-flight response."
~ Deepak Chopra

Stress is the illness of our age. Many people are trying to do more in less time. The difficulty comes when these people are not able to cope. Stress is not caused by the situation but rather their reaction to the situation. Have you ever seen one person who was very stressed while another person in the same situation was not stressed?

Fight or flight was a great tool when we lived in caves and were hunted by lions. In today's world the triggers are not life threatening, but people react in the same way. And that is the problem, reacting rather than responding.

When you are faced with a situation and you feel anxiety start to build, the first thing to do is stop. Stop, relax, take a deep breath or two, and think of a response. When you stop, you can eliminate your initial stressful reaction and allow yourself to come up with an appropriate action.

When your body realizes it is not in immediate physical danger, the fight or flight reaction goes away and stress is averted. The more you can practice this, the easier it will be.

Today respond instead of reacting.

July 15

"Our every thought, image, or affirmation is a prayer. Therefore, if everything you think, feel, say or do is a form of prayer, then make it uplifted and exalted."
~ Mark Victor Hansen

Imagine how you would act if everyone you talked to were God.

Would you be polite?
Would you be nice?
Would you be generous?

Since God is everywhere and everything, then everyone you talk to is a part of God. We are all children of God, and the name you have for God does not matter. We are all connected, so when you are loving to someone else, you are loving to yourself.

All of your thoughts and words have power. Make sure you use that power for your highest good. If you have a negative thought, replace it with a loving thought. Then repeat the loving thought ten times until the negativity is gone. Feel the love and joy flowing from you as you do this, and make your world a loving place.

Today let your life be an uplifted and exalted prayer.

July 16

"Eighty percent of success is showing up."~ Woody Allen

Or as I heard Will Smith say, "When you're ready, you don't have to get ready." All people have dreams and desires. They are hoping for some great opportunity, but when the opportunity shows up, they often miss it. They are not ready because they didn't show up that day.

When you start each day ready for whatever happens and looking for the great opportunity, your chances of finding it and being able to act on it are greater. If you are an actor, you should have a current head shot with you and be ready to give it to the right person. If you are a business owner, you should be ready to give a thirty second pitch about your business. Have business cards made. Put up a website. Look and act your best every time you leave the house.

Look for the opportunities, and then be ready to act on them when they show up. If you knew that today was the day your opportunity was going to show up, how would you dress? How would you act? What would you take with you? How would you prepare? Think about this and then every day do those things until your opportunity shows up. Then get ready for the next opportunity.

Today show up and be ready.

July 17
"A great man is always willing to be little."
~ Ralph Waldo Emerson

Greatness comes in many forms, and I believe we are all capable of being great. The men and women who have realized their greatness often have one thing in common. Once they have realized they are great, they give up trying to convince other people that they are great.

When you know you are great, you don't care what other people think. Your opinion of yourself does not rely on the opinions of others. Remember that Jesus washed his disciples' feet. People who spend time trying to impress other people are usually trying to convince themselves that they are special.

Look for people who are modest about their achievements. These are the people who are often the greatest. Then learn to be modest yourself.

Today look for the greatness around you.

July 18
"Power is of two kinds. One is obtained by the fear of punishment and the other by acts of love. Power based on love is a thousand times more effective and permanent than the one derived from fear of punishment."
~ Mohandas Gandhi

When a leader rules by fear, the people he rules will look for a new leader and try to escape his rule at every chance. This is true for leaders of nations, companies, and households.

When you lead with love, with the purpose of helping those you lead, you will find loyalty. We all assume the role of leadership at one time or another. When you do, express love, and help those you are leading to better themselves.

When you eliminate fear, you allow the people you lead to be more creative. You allow them to be themselves.

Today allow those you lead to have freedom from fear, and you may find that your fear will also go away.

July 19

"Kind words can be short and easy to speak, but their echoes are truly endless."~ Mother Teresa

Kind words can have a profound effect on people. Not only what you say but how you say it is important. Often in our busy lives we forget that the people we interact with have feelings just like we do.

Take the time to say nice things and be nice to everyone, not just the people you live with and work with. Be kind to cashiers, waiters, and even other drivers. Be kind in actions and words, and then watch how your world transforms into a kinder place to live. Your kindness and love will make the world a better place, not just for you, but for everyone.

Today be nice to everyone you meet.

July 20

"No one is safe on the planet until all of the hate is gone."
~ The Scary Guy

Hate, anger, fear, prejudice, and judgement hurt us all. When you walk into a room full of angry people, it is hard not get angry. And when someone is angry or mean toward you, the common response is to return that anger with anger. But doing that only allows the flow of anger to continue.

The only way to remove hate from the world is to respond with love. I know this is probably the hardest thing in the world to do, but it can be done. Don't give in to anger and hatred. Learn to respect and accept everyone. Even if you can't immediately respond with love, don't let the flow of hate continue.

Today answer hatred with love.

July 21

"One word frees us of all the weight and pain of life. That word is love."~ Sophocles

Pain comes from a lack of love. When you can give love in a situation, the pain goes away. Love can be in the form of gratitude, appreciation, respect, or caring. However you express love is up to you. When you feel anger, resentment, or jealousy in a situation, you are causing pain for yourself.

You are the cause of all of your pain. When you accept that responsibility, then, and only then, can you take control of your life. Give love in every situation and your life will transform.

I know this sounds simple, but most truths are simple. When you live this, you will live a new life.

Today give love in every situation.

July 22

"The secret of success in life is for a man to be ready for his opportunity when it comes."~ Benjamin Disraeli

Opportunities are all around you. Some are better than others, but all are there for the taking. You just need to be ready.

Think about what you would like to have in your life. If that opportunity were available right now, would you be ready to take it?

If you know you want to get rid of your car and get a new one, is your old car ready to be traded in, or is it full of trash ? Do you know where the title is? Do you have space in your garage for your new car? If you want to get rid of your old car, be ready to let go of it to make way for a new one.

If you want a romantic relationship, have you prepared yourself, your mind, and your home to accept someone new in your life? When you go out, are you ready to meet someone? If you are looking for a business deal, are you ready to do the deal today?

Decide what you want, get ready for the opportunity, and then anticipate it. Then when the opportunity arises, you will be ready to act on it.

Today get ready for what you want.

July 23

"Too may people overvalue what they are not and undervalue what they are."~ Malcolm Forbes

You are a great person, and you have amazing skills. Focus on using your skills and don't concern yourself with the skills other people have. Other people are not better than you, they are just different.

Focus on what you are good at doing. You can do things that no one else can do, and you do them in your own special way.

Stop undervaluing yourself and your abilities. Don't compare yourself to others. Appreciate yourself for who you are. Give yourself a pat on the back for being the wonderful, talented person you are.

Today know that you are great.

July 24

"The purpose of our lives is to be happy."~ Dalai Lama

This can be a life changing idea. Most people believe life's purpose is to succeed at one thing or another. We are constantly striving to get somewhere, and when we arrive, we decide we need to go somewhere else. Believing that we are here to be happy changes things.

It brings up the question, can I be happy right here, right now? And the answer is yes. When you release the desire to be in a different place or have different things, then you can indeed be happy. And isn't that what you really want? Isn't the reason you are trying to get to that next place because you believe that is where happiness is? Well, I can tell you happiness is there, but happiness is also where you are now. Your happiness is inside you. You just need to allow it to come out.

Today release the need to get somewhere and be just be happy now.

July 25

"Selfishness is not living as one wishes to live, it is asking others to live as one wishes to live."~ Oscar Wilde

When I read this it instantly became one of my favorite quotes. I have a strong will, and I am true to my beliefs and true to myself, but I never considered myself to be selfish because I don't insist that other people agree with me or live their lives according to my standards.

Many people, however, do go through life insisting that other people do things to make them happy. When those demands are not met, their reactions can range from annoyance to anger to guilt to self pity. All of these are just tools people use to get what they want, tools they use to impose their will on others.

Imagine going through life without demanding anything of anyone else. Imagine allowing the people around you to live the way they want to live. Do you think the people around you would enjoy the freedom?

As a manager or a boss, you get to set the rules and the expectations, but allow your team to work within that framework as they see fit.

The same is true in your personal life. We all have rules and expectations of how we wish to be treated, and we do not have to allow others to infringe on our freedom or our ability to choose, but by the same token, we cannot infringe on another's freedom or his ability to choose. Allow others to be themselves and accept them for who they are. It's okay if your friends and family members make decisions that are different than yours. Allow people the freedom to be who they are, and they will love you for it.

Today allow the people around you to be themselves.

July 26

"I would rather be loathed for who I am than loved for who I am not."~ Wayne Dyer

For many people life is a popularity contest. They are constantly trying to fit in, seek approval, or be part of the in crowd. This is obvious in high school, but it continues later in life, too. Many people think they need the right clothes, or the right car, or the right house, or the right job. For many this becomes a trap. They spend so much time trying to fit in that they loose who they are, and then their relationships are based on a false idea of who they are. But it doesn't have to be that way.

True happiness can be discovered when you are true to yourself. When you stop playing the game, you may loose some friends, but if they cannot accept you for who you are, they were not true friends anyway. Be true to yourself, and the people who show up in your life will love you for you. Understand that people who cannot accept you may still be learning to accept themselves. Their opinion of you cannot hurt you.

Today be yourself.

July 27
"The art of living lies less in eliminating our troubles than in growing with them."~ Bernard M. Baruch

Our greatest trouble often reveals our greatest opportunity, but often we miss it. When we experience troubles or setbacks, we are often focused on the hardship and miss the blessing.

After a layoff, instead of taking the time to explore new and different opportunities, we sit and complain that it wasn't fair. We focus on how wrong it was rather than seeing the new adventure that has just shown up. Stop looking at the problem and find the benefit.

The difference between successful people and unsuccessful people is that successful people are constantly looking for the next opportunity and learning from their last problem.

Today if a problem arises, use it to see how you can grow.

July 28

"Live today. Not yesterday. Not tomorrow. Just today. Inhabit your moments. Don't rent them out to tomorrow."
~ Jerry Spinelli

Today is what matters. Now is what matters. Focus on what you are doing. Do one thing, focus on that one thing, and keep at it until you are finished. Don't think about the party this weekend or the party last weekend. Just focus on the task at hand. When you do this, you will finish quickly, and you will do a better job.

The same is true in relationships. Focus on the person you are talking to. Listen to what he is saying, and when he is finished, then think of what you want to say.

Focus on the person you are talking to. Focus on the task you are doing. Focus on this moment.

Today wherever you are be there.

July 29

"If we will be quiet and ready enough, we shall find compensation in every disappointment."
~ Henry David Thoreau

Disappointment comes from how you look at a situation. When you have expectations that are not met, you choose to be disappointed. When you step back from those moments, the view can change. Where you saw disappointment and upset, an opportunity will emerge. There may be a lesson in the event or a chance to do something new.

When you are upset or disappointed, sit in a quiet room. Clear your mind, and after a few minutes ask, what is the compensation? Then remain quiet until the answer comes. Usually it will appear. If it doesn't, try this again a little later. Learn to let go of your negative emotions. Only then will the opportunities arise.

Once you see the opportunity, act on it, and act quickly. So many wonderful gifts are never received because the recipient waited too long to accept them.

Today turn a disappointment into an advantage.

July 30

"He who is not contented with what he has would not be contented with what he would like to have."~ Socrates

Contentment is not a matter of what you have, but your perception about what you have. A person who has no shelter from the rain would be very content in a small tent, while a person who is used to living in a mansion may find the tent unbearable.

When people want more and get it, they quickly go back to wanting more. I agree that striving to better yourself is a great thing to do, but don't sacrifice your happiness to do it. Be happy and content where you are with what you have. Work for what you desire, but don't allow the desire to consume you. Be thankful and grateful right now.

Today count your blessings, know that you have enough, and be happy.

July 31

"One forgives to the degree that one loves."
~ Francois de La Rochefoucauld

Most people think that when they forgive, they are doing something for someone else. This is not true. When you forgive, you are giving a gift to yourself. So it is not how much you love another, but how much you love yourself that is important. When you love yourself, you're more open to forgiving because deep down you know that all forgiveness is self forgiveness.

When you love yourself, it is easier to forgive. When you hold on to resentment, you feel anger. The more you love yourself, the less you want to feel this anger. The more you love yourself, the easier it is to forgive. And the more you forgive, the more you can love.

Today learn to love yourself, be forgiving, and learn to forgive by loving.

August 1

"Happiness is a choice."~ Mark Rose

Happiness is indeed a choice. When events happen in your life, you get to choose how you will react. You decide what meaning you will give the events. If you don't believe me, think about how you would feel if someone has his car stolen.

Then think about how you would feel if your car was stolen. Same event, different reactions.

You have the ability to choose love in any situation, and the result of choosing love is happiness. When you first start this you may still react with anger or fear to some events. If that happens, notice your emotion and bring love to the situation. Try to gain understanding. At first this may be hard, but it will become easier, and soon your natural reaction will be love. When you choose love, your life will become one of happiness and peace.

Many of the greatest teachers have chosen love when faced with hatred. Jesus, Ghandi, Dr. Martin Luther King Jr., Mother Theresa, and Bishop Desmond Tutu all chose love and happiness, and so can you.

Today take the first step. Choose to be happy and have a great day.

August 2
"You do not become good by trying to be good, but by finding the goodness that is already within you and allowing that goodness to emerge."~ Eckhart Tolle

Your true nature is to be good, happy, and loving. If you are not feeling these feelings, it is not because you are not good, it is because something is blocking your good from coming forth.

When you are sick, the virus or bacteria is keeping your good health from coming through. When the pathogen is removed, your good health emerges. When you are unhappy, you need to remove what is blocking your happiness so you can be happy again. These blocks usually show up in the form of beliefs. You believe that you need something you don't have to be happy. You believe you need to act a certain way to be accepted. Change what you believe about yourself and your world will change.

If someone else thinks you are bad, mean, or unhappy, that is their belief and does not concern you. What matters is how you feel about yourself.

Today look at what you believe about yourself and change just one belief so you can let your true self out.

August 3

"No man becomes rich unless he enriches others."
~ Andrew Carnegie

This can be taken two ways. First, to gain wealth you must help others to become wealthy, and I think this is true. But the deeper meaning is that by enriching the lives of others we gain more than money could ever buy.

The true riches that are the joys of a happy life are health, friends, and a relationship with God. To experience these great pleasures, we need only do one thing. Enrich the lives of those around us. Give more than you take from the people you come in contact with. You can give a smile or an encouraging word. You can give your time or your knowledge. Just give.

Many people work hard with the goal of buying their happiness or at least buying things that they feel will make them happy. The secret is that happiness comes from giving.

Today enrich someone's life, and your life will be enriched.

August 4

"A first-rate soup is more creative than a second-rate painting."~ Abraham Maslow

People often confuse fame with greatness. There are many great people who have become famous, but these two qualities are not linked. You can be great and not famous, or famous and not great. When you express your creativity, you allow your greatness to show through. We cannot all be great painters, but we can all be great at something.

Wherever you are and whatever you are doing, do your best. Don't settle for second-rate from yourself. Maybe someone else can do better than your best, and that is okay as long as you know that you did your best. I have always said, "I would rather have C work from a C employee, than B work from an A employee."

Do what you love and do it the best that you can and then share your work. You may become famous with your paintings, or you may have friends over for a nice bowl of soup. Either way make it great.

Today do your best.

August 5

"Nothing occurs in your life - nothing - which is not first a thought. Thoughts are like magnets, drawing effects to you." ~ Neale Donald Walsch

Everything started as a thought. Every invention and every great accomplishment was once just a thought in the mind of one person.

What are you thinking? What are you spending your time focusing on? If you like where you are in your life, then keep thinking about what you have been thinking about. If you would like to change where you are in life, then change your thoughts. Focus on what you want. Focus on the good, and be grateful for all you have.

Today pay attention to where your mind goes, and focus on the good.

August 6

"We make a living by what we get. We make a life by what we give." ~ Sir Winston Churchill

Making a living can be important. We need food, shelter, and clothing. Making a living allows these needs to be met. The key is not to give up your life while making a living.

Making a life involves doing what you love and using that talent to enrich the lives of other people. A person's greatness is judged by what he gives, not what he has. The most amazing thing is when you give something that has real value such as love, kindness, help, encouragement, or friendship, you get the same in return. The more love you give, the more you get, and the greater you become. The world becomes a little more loving and we all benefit from that.

The same principal is true with abundance. When you can live a life enriching others, you will be enriched. When you can spread abundance, you will be abundant.

Today give of yourself. Give to those close to you and give to strangers, even if it's only a smile.

August 7

"People who think too much before they act don't act too much."~ Jimmy Buffett

Many people are stuck. They don't do anything because they are not sure what direction they should go. They examine a situation for so long that by the time they buy an 8-track player, everyone else has an iPod.

If you only take action when you know it is a sure thing, you will miss many of the great opportunities that come your way. Sure, some chances you take may turn out bad, but that's okay. Learn from your mistakes and take another chance. I am not advising you to do everything. Examine your options. Then go with your gut instinct.

The world is moving and changing at a faster pace than it ever has before. The people who enjoy the most success are the ones who can make decisions quickly, those who can seize an opportunity before it disappears.

Today remember it is better to strike out swinging than never to play the game.

August 8
"Never discourage anyone...who continually makes progress, no matter how slow."~ Plato

So many people are stagnant that you need to encourage those who are moving forward. Remember the tortoise won the race.

Slow and steady progress has a way of sneaking up on you. Slow and steady will often get things done much faster than you expect. Remember this when thinking about others as well as yourself.

Do you have a big project to finish? Break it down into little bits and see how quickly you finish. A big project will be much easier to complete when you make it a series of little projects.

Today encourage all progress, even yours.

August 9
"Maxim for life: You get treated in life the way you teach people to treat you."~ Wayne Dyer

When we interact with other people, we establish rules and boundaries. These are the rules that we expect others to live by when they interact with us. These rules allow us to have boundaries. If the people we spend time with don't live by the rules we have, we don't have to allow them in our lives.

There are two things to watch out for in this process. First, if your rules are too lax, you can be used and abused by others. Second, if your rules are too strict, no one will want to be around you.

Be sure you communicate your rules to the people in your life. If they break your rules, explain the rules to them nicely, but be sure you are not trying to dictate how they live, just how they interact with you. If a person chooses to use vulgar language, that is his choice. You can tell him that if he wants to spend time with you that vulgarity is not acceptable. In this way you are not telling him how to live, but rather telling him how you expect to be treated.

Today examine the rules you have, and if someone breaks them, explain your position to him in a nice way.

August 10
"Life is not war, and people are not the enemy."~ Unknown

In this country we have waged war on just about everything from drugs to crime to terrorism to poverty to greed. A Google search even shows a war on Christmas, kids, and condoms. We are so quick to declare this group or that group the enemy. People want to fight against everything they do not agree with.

Let's change our point of view. When we disagree with something, let's try to understand it and learn to accept it. By accepting it, you can move to a place where you have the opportunity to affect a change. Instead of declaring a war on drugs, help one person kick the habit.

Instead of fighting a war, practice giving love. When you love someone, you allow him to see how wonderful he really is. You allow his divine nature to come through. When you realize that we are all connected and that we are all in this together, then you know that there is no one to fight.

Today change the world by changing yourself. Be the best you can be. Be kind and loving. Then you can help someone else be the same way.

August 11
"People living deeply have no fear of death."~ Anais Nin

When you live your life to the fullest, death is less of a concern. When you do everything you can every day, you won't die wishing you had done more.

Tell the people you love how you feel. Do the things you've always wanted to do, and do them as soon as you can. I am not saying to go into debt or ignore the future, but make the most of this moment. Enjoy this moment. Forget about the past. Don't worry about the future. Forgive everyone now and have fun.

Today, right here, right now, smile and enjoy yourself.

August 12

"Everybody has their own ideas of Shangri-La....I tried to teach myself to enjoy the present, enjoy the now."
~ Mark Knopfler

Now is when everything happens. You can remember the past and dream about the future, but all of the action, all of the fun, is here and now.

A happy life is full of happy moments, and the only moment you can enjoy is now. You can be happy in the future, but not until it gets here, and when it gets here, it will be now.

Learn to let go of the past and focus on now. And if you want the best for your future, remember that the actions you take now are what determine how your future will unfold. You are meant to be happy. Shangri-La, Heaven, and Nirvana are all right here, right now. You just need to realize it to see it.

Today accept happiness now.

August 13

"Whenever you're facing any form of resistance, gratitude has the power to quickly dissolve it. This is true whether the hindrance comes from inside of you or outside of you."
~ Peggy McColl

When you learn to be grateful for what you have, life becomes easier. Be grateful for the resistance. Be grateful for the problem. You may not see the benefit now, but know it is there. Be thankful for everything.

After experiencing gratitude, ask, what is the lesson I am to learn here? If you do not receive an answer, that is okay. If you do receive an answer, be sure to learn the lesson so the next time a similar issue arises, you will know how to take care of it.

Today be grateful.

August 14

"The love that you withhold is the pain that you carry."
~ Vasais

Love is amazing. The more you give the more you have, but the opposite is true as well. The more you withhold the less you have. When you give love, your pain goes away. When you are angry at someone or you hold a grudge, the pain is in you not the other person. When you give someone love, you experience the love more than the other person does.

Let go of your pain, forgive, and move on. Love everyone and feel the love grow inside you. You do not have to like everyone in your life, but love them all the same.

Today let go of the pain. Give love.

August 15

"Don't tell people they can do the impossible. Tell people that they can do the possible that they think is impossible."
~ Denis Waitley

So often we defeat ourselves before we ever get started. We believe that a task is impossible, so we never start. I think about the construction of Stonehenge. Those people quarried huge rocks by hand, moved them over 200 miles, and then erected them. Think about how long it took just to find the place to dig up the stones. They worked on this for hundreds of years. But they did it.

I have no idea how long it took to get just one stone moved. It could have been a lifetime of work to set just one stone, but they knew the only way to get it done was to get started. I think that many people in today's fast food/microwave world of instant gratification are unwilling to start something unless they can finish it today or this week. If it can't be finished right away, it is deemed impossible.

Look at the things you would like to accomplish and start working on the biggest one. Take one step in the direction you wish to go. Then tomorrow take another step. You may find that the task is easier than you thought, but you will never know until you start moving.

Today start something that seemed impossible yesterday.

August 16

"The one thing all famous authors, world class athletes, business tycoons, singers, actors, and celebrated achievers in any field have in common is that they all began their journeys when they were none of these things. Yet still, they began their journeys."~ Mike Dooley

You take journeys every day, and you cannot see the destination from the starting point. Most of us can't see the grocery store from our house, yet we take that trip easily. It is an easy trip because it is one we have made before. We know the destination and the route.

The journey to greatness in our lives is harder to see. It is a trip many of us have not made before. But just like going to Disney World or England or New York for the first time, other people have made the journey successfully, and we will find all of the help we need along the way to reach our destination successfully, too.

Today start your journey to greatness, and the help you need will find you.

August 17

"Any person who contributes to prosperity must prosper in turn."~ Earl Nightingale

To be prosperous you need the right mindset, and then you need to take action. Help other people become wealthy, and you will become wealthy too. Help other people to have more free time, and you will have more free time too.

Today ask yourself, "How can I be of service?" Help others even if they have no way to repay you.

August 18

"Sell your cleverness and purchase bewilderment."~ Rumi

I believe the message Rumi wanted us to take from this is that the world is much more interesting when we don't have it all figured out.

Think about a small child. Everything is an adventure, from picking dandelions to throwing rocks into a pond. Everything is new, exciting, and fun.

Now think about your life. How often do you have new experiences? When was the last time you were amazed or bewildered?

Try to see things with new eyes. Notice the world around you. When you see a tree, take time to really look at it. Look at it as if you have never seen a tree before. When you see a person, try to see him as if for the first time. See who he truly is, not who you think he is, and allow him to be himself.

Today allow yourself to be bewildered.

August 19

"Insecurity is the result of trying to be secure."~ Alan Watts

So many people are trying to be safe. They invest their money and time with the idea of not losing instead of investing with the idea of winning. They stay in jobs and relationships because they are comfortable or safe. While trying to avoid risk, the opportunity for real gain is missed. We all know who Christopher Columbus is because he risked sailing off the edge of the world. Had he stayed on the shore, he would not be remembered.

What we think of as secure often isn't really secure at all. In recent years, many people who thought they had a safe and secure job found themselves unemployed. The people who were willing to stand out from the crowd and do something new may have gotten fired, or they may be on the way up. Be in control of your own destiny instead of leaving your future to someone else.

Many people are afraid of change. The problem is that the world is constantly changing. You can cause the change or you can sit by and watch things change. When you cause the change, you have a better idea of where it's going and how to make the change work for you.

Today do something different, something risky. The more you do this the safer you will be.

August 20
"Don't make the mistake of thinking that concerned people cannot change the world; it is the only thing that ever has."
~ Margaret Mead

Big changes start with little ideas. An idea in the mind of one person can spread to another person, and another, until it becomes a movement. A movement causes more people to take action, and the next thing you know, the world has changed, but it all started with one person and one thought.

You may not have aspirations of changing the world, but you can change the world in which you live. The movement you begin may only affect your immediate family, but if you want things to change, the first step is to have a thought.

Today think of something great.

August 21

"Happiness is not something ready made. It comes from your own actions." ~ Dalai Lama

Notice that his holiness didn't say happiness comes from the actions of others. You control your happiness. If you choose to be happy, you will remain happy until you decide otherwise. The catch is that often we make these decisions subconsciously. Our own actions, actions we perform again and again, or re-actions, are why we get mad or grumpy. We do it out of habit.

But now that you are aware of this, you can change your mood. When you find yourself feeling something you don't want to feel, know that you have the power to change how you feel. Decide to be happy or peaceful, or you can even decide to be mad, but remember the decision is entirely yours, so don't blame other people for how you feel. Take responsibility for your mood and your life.

No one has the power to choose your mood except you. When you say something makes you happy, the truth is that when that something or someone is present, you decide to be happy. Your happiness is always your decision.

Today take back the control of your life by taking control of your mood.

August 22

"Learn all you can from the mistakes of others. You won't have time to make them all yourself."~ Alfred Sheinwold

We all make mistakes, and we hope we can learn from them so we can more easily get the results we want. This is a good plan, but it will only take you part of the way. Time is working against you. You can speed up the process if you learn from others. Often the most valuable lessons come when we are faced with large decisions, and the ramifications of making a wrong choice regarding a large decision can be huge.

For example, if you buy a house to flip, you could end up with a gold mine or a money pit. An experienced eye can tell the difference between the two. So study. Study the people who have been down the road you want to travel. Read about the lives of the people you wish to emulate and learn from their experiences. Then talk to people who can help you and follow their advice. Then when you reach the top, become a mentor. When you learn from the mistakes of others, you open the door to success.

Today learn from someone else's mistakes.

August 23

"Self confidence is knowing that you are wonderful. Arrogance is thinking you are better than someone else."
~ Mark Rose

There is nothing wrong with thinking you are great. In fact knowing that you are great and wonderful is an amazing place to be. The problem comes when we think we are better than other people.

All of us have special talents. Everyone has something that he or she is great at doing. So if you compare yourself to another, you may see that you have more skill in a particular area than another person. But I am quite sure there is some area where the other person is more skilled.

To increase your self worth, just know that you were created in the image and likeness of God. You are a wonderful, beautiful person. Now that you know that, stop comparing yourself to others. You can work to improve yourself and look at other people as models of what is possible, but don't ever think that because one person has achieved more in one area of his life that he is better than you. We are all equally wonderful. It is just expressed differently in all of us.

Today, know that you are wonderful, and everyone else is wonderful too.

August 24

"If you love what you do you'll never work another day in your life."~ Mark Twain

Most people spend half of their waking hours at work, traveling to and from work, and thinking about work. Why spend half of your life miserable? Do what you love and love what you do. When you love your job, your entire world is better. You are happier, you are nicer to your family, you complain less, and you have less stress.

When you are in a job you don't like, you can change jobs or change your attitude. To change your attitude, focus on the good aspects of your job. Every job has good points. List all of the reasons you like your job and then focus on them and feel grateful that you have a job and an income. When you have gratitude for what you have, you open yourself up for more.

After you change your attitude, ask yourself, "Am I doing what I love?" If not, start to move in that direction. The key is appreciating what you have before you look for something new.

Today have fun at work.

August 25

"Destiny is not a matter of chance, it is a matter of choice; it is not a thing to be waited for, it is a thing to be achieved."
~ William Jennings Bryant

When you figure out what your destiny is, get busy working on it. Many times people know what their destiny is, what their life's purpose is, but they don't move in that direction. They are stuck waiting for the perfect time. Stop waiting.

If you know your life's purpose, then you know where you want to go, so start moving in that direction. Stop making excuses and start taking action. The only way to fulfill your life's purpose is to get out there and do something about it.

Today figure out where life wants you to go and start moving in that direction.

August 26

"If you have much—give of your wealth. If you have little—give of your heart."~ Arab Proverb

We all have something to give, and giving keeps us in the flow of life. As we give, we are sending a message to the universe that we are thankful and that we want to return the generosity that the universe has given us. When we are thankful, the universe gives us more.

Think of it like this. If you give one child a bag of M&M's and she shares that gift with her brother, you are happy to give her more. However, if she refuses to share her candy, you may take some of what she has and give it to her brother. She will feel as if the candy was stolen, and you will be reluctant to give her candy in the future.

The universe works in the same way. When you give, you open yourself to receive. When you share the blessings that you have received, the universe is happy to share more blessings with you.

Today give something.

August 27

"I have learned that if one advances confidently in the direction of his dreams and endeavors to live the life he has imagined, he will meet with a success unexpected in common hours."~ Henry David Thoreau

What is your dream?

You have to have a dream or a goal before you can move toward that dream.

Most people would rather say, "I could have played in the NFL if I had really tried," instead of, "I gave it my all but I wasn't good enough." Most people want an excuse, an out. They would rather live a mediocre life then try their best and risk failing.

Thinking like this is what's keeping you from ever realizing your dream. Take the risk, put all of your chips on the table, believe in what you want, and do what it takes to make it happen. Your dream was placed inside you by God, so trust that God will help you make it happen.

Many great journeys start with a leap of faith.

Today start to work toward your dream.

August 28

"The tragedy in life doesn't lie in not reaching your goal. The tragedy lies in having no goal to reach."~ Benjamin E. Mays

This is important to remember just after you reach a goal. As you achieve the things you want, enjoy them and be happy. Then look for your next goal. If you have $1,000,000 in the bank, your goal could be to have $2,000,000, or it could be to spend more time with your family. You get to choose the direction your life will go, but when you don't choose a direction, you are not likely to go anywhere.

Today chose the direction you want to go by setting a goal.

August 29

"By all means listen to other people's advice, but when in doubt go with your gut instinct."~ Steve Pavlina

Advice can be a great tool, but it is only a tool. We are all different. We all have different wants and desires and are willing to put up with different things. Something that aggravates a friend of yours may not bother you, and vice versa.

Listen to the advice of others and see if it feels right to you, not if it makes logical sense, but if it feels right. Then go with your gut. Your instincts are better than you give them credit for being. Always trust your gut feelings. Get the advice, listen to the opinions of others, then do what feels right to you.

Today trust your gut.

August 30

"He who is of a calm and happy nature will hardly feel the pressure of age, but to him who is of an opposite disposition, youth and age are equally a burden."~ Plato

When you choose to be happy, you realize that you are the perfect age. You are neither too old nor too young. Your age is just a number that counts the amount of times you have circled the sun.

When you do not choose to be happy, your age becomes an excuse. You are either too old or too young to be where you want to be or do what you want to do. You blame your age because it sounds more like a reason than an excuse, but it is still an excuse.

Today give up the excuse of your age and decide to be happy now.

August 31

"Nothing is either good or bad, but thinking makes it so."
~ William Shakespeare

This can be difficult to agree with because you always see the world from your point of view. Even when you try to see things in a different way, the information is still processed by your brain. The way you perceive the world determines if an event is good or bad.

The stock market goes down and you loose money, but someone else now has an opportunity to buy low. A car accident produces revenue for the body shop, and a natural disaster could be the kick in the pants someone needed to change his or her life.

When you change the way you look at things, you open up to new possibilities. Problems become opportunities. Disappointments become sources of inspiration. And upsets become happy moments.

When you realize that you are upset, try to see the situation in a different way. Ask yourself, what is the good in the situation? Ask yourself how you can see the situation differently. Then you can look at events from the past and examine them so you can turn old upsets into positive memories.

Today realize that all is well.

September 1

"Cruelty towards others is always also cruelty towards ourselves."~ Paul Tillich

Most cruelty comes from fear, envy, and a lack of self esteem. The more you love yourself, the nicer you are to other people.

When someone says something mean to you, he is likely trying to feel better about himself by putting you down. This doesn't work. He may even feel bad for being mean, yet continue to be mean because he doesn't realize he's only hurting himself. It could also be he feels threatened by you.

When someone is mean or cruel to you, your first reaction may be to retaliate. This may satisfy your ego, but it won't help you. Be strong and know that what he is saying has everything to do with him and nothing to do with you. Send him love and let his comments run off you like water off a duck's back.

Today rise above cruelty.

September 2

"Abundance doesn't follow giving until giving is its own reward."~ Jan Denise

So many great figures in history have advised people to do what they love and do what they do for the sake of doing it. When the task is the reward, the outcome becomes unimportant. When the outcome is unimportant, you are no longer relying on other people's opinions but rather on your own sense of accomplishment.

When you give, do you expect a thank you? Do you want some recognition? Does the act of giving enrich you, or is it the recognition of the act of giving that enriches you? When you get to the point where giving is its own reward, then you open yourself up to abundance. It sounds ironic, but by giving freely you are sending the message that you have enough, and the law of attraction responds by giving you more than enough. When you give with the idea of wanting something in return, you get more wanting.

Today give something to someone who can't pay you back. Give your time, your kindness, your love, or your money. Just give.

September 3

"There is nothing wrong when men possess riches. The wrong comes when riches possess men."~ Billy Graham.

Having nice things is great. Having enough money to do whatever you want to do is awesome. The question is are you a slave to your possessions? Are you always trying to get more instead of being thankful for what you have? Are you focused on getting more or helping more?

The people who live the most fulfilled lives spend their time helping others. This doesn't mean you need to be Mother Theresa. Bill Gates and Donald Trump have both contributed to the world and helped millions of people. When you focus on giving and helping, you end up getting more in return.

Today focus on helping others and be thankful for what you have.

September 4

"How does one become a butterfly? You must want to fly so much that you are willing to give up being a caterpillar."
~ Trina Paulus

Do you want to fly? Is there something that you really want in your life? Are you willing to give up who you are now to grow into this new identity?

For example, would you be willing to give up being sick to be healthy? If you said yes, think about what you must give up. Your poor health will no longer be an excuse for not doing something. You will get no more sympathy for being sick.

You will have to let go of all your negative beliefs about health issues. But, you will be free from colds, headaches, allergy attacks, or any other *dis-ease* you now believe you can suffer from. Your body will no longer be a limitation.

If you have health issues, pay attention to how often you talk about your poor health. Think about the sympathy you get. Think about the things you ask others to do for you because you are limited by your body. When you give all that up, then you will become a healthy person. But you must start doing the things a healthy person does. *See* yourself as healthy, strong, and well.

Today decide what you want to become and start to give up your old identity.

September 5

"I believe that anyone can conquer fear by doing the things he fears to do, provided he keeps doing them until he gets a record of successful experience behind him."
~ Eleanor Roosevelt

Most fears are unfounded, and if you are living in fear, you are not living in love.

Look at the things you are afraid of doing, and make plans to do one of those things. It could be skydiving or holding a snake. You may be afraid of being in a crowd or speaking in front of a group. Whatever it is, do it. Then continue to do it until you can do it successfully without fear.

When you have overcome one fear, it will be easier to overcome other fears. Soon you will be living your life accomplishing what you want without the shadow of fear hanging over you.

Today face your fears.

September 6

"You have enemies? Good. That means you've stood up for something, sometime in your life."~ Winston Churchill

It is great to be popular and well liked, but if everyone always agrees with you, you are not saying anything of substance. Do not try to make people angry, but tell people your thoughts when they ask. Be considerate of others' feelings, but be honest. Then if they disagree, that is fine. You can have friends with different opinions.

Today stand up for what you believe, and allow others to stand up for what they believe too.

September 7

"If you want to see what children can do, you must stop giving them things."~ Norman Douglas

Children have great imaginations. This can be a great asset or a detriment. Imagination is an asset because children can go places adults never see. They can create friends and experiences that are wonderful and amazing. And if they can keep this imagination until adulthood, it will help them create a life full of wonder and amazement.

However, kids today have less free time than ever to use their imaginations. And the fantasy worlds of TV and video games become the places they go when they imagine. Consequently, they lose the ability to imagine new experiences for themselves. Let your kids have time to themselves without looking at a screen. Allow them to use their imaginations, and when they invite you into their fantasy world, go with them.

Kids who don't have toys will find something to play with. If they have never had to do this before, they will resist, but sooner or later their imaginations will kick in, and they will play.

Today let your kids have some free time to explore their minds.

September 8

"People rarely succeed unless they have fun in what they are doing."~ Dale Carnegie

People who hate their jobs and are living for the weekend miss the great opportunities in life. When you have fun and enjoy doing what you are doing, you bring an energy to it that is unlike anything else. You can't fake that energy. You either have it or you don't, and you know if it is there. You know that feeling you get when you are doing something you love? That feeling is the energy.

When that energy is present, you are able to be more successful because of that energy. That energy is your connection with your Divine source. That connection allows you to do more with less and have more fun while you are doing it.

Today do what you love and have fun doing it.

September 9

"What has made me successful is the ability to surrender my plans, dreams, and goals to a power that's greater than other people and greater than myself."~ Oprah Winfrey

Let go and let God.

But what if God's plans don't fit me?

What if God wants me to do something I don't want to do?

What if God wants me to renounce wealth, abundance, and intimacy?

God knows what your desires are. God knows everything about you and wants the best for you. It is hard to let go, but if you are able to let go, then you will be able to experience the greatness of God.

Think about what you have created and what God has created. If you conclude that God thinks on a larger scale, then allow God to take over one part of your life. Just one part. Then see how it goes. Then I'm sure you will be more than willing to give over the rest.

Today let go and let God.

September 10

"Birthdays are nature's way of telling us to eat more cake."
~ Unknown

"Birthdays are good for you. Statistics show that the people who have the most live the longest."
~ Reverend Larry Lorenzoni

Welcome each new day and make the most of it. How you feel about your age is your choice. You can feel young at 80 or old at 25. Your worth is not determined by how many trips you have taken around the sun but by how much love you give.

Today give love, ignore your age, and eat a piece of cake.

September 11

"The basic thing is that everyone wants happiness, no one wants suffering. And happiness mainly comes from our own attitude rather than from external factors. If your own mental attitude is correct, even if you remain in a hostile atmosphere, you feel happy."~ Dalai Lama

Happiness is a choice. You can choose to be happy, or you can let the world around you determine your mood.

By choosing to be happy, your life is under your control. You can transform the world you live in rather than the world you live in transforming you.

Today watch your attitude and choose to be happy.

September 12

"Everything has beauty, but not everyone sees it."
~ Confucius

As you go through your day, try to see the beauty all around you. Look for the perfection in nature. Beauty is everywhere. You just have to open up your mind to see it. Give up your labels of things and see them for what they are.

When you see beauty and perfection everywhere, life just seems to work better because you are focusing on the good, and as a result, more good will show up in your life. If you are looking for beauty and perfection, you will find beauty and perfection.

Today look for the beauty in your world.

September 13

"Failure lies not in falling down. Failure lies in not getting up."~ Chinese Proverb

Imagine parents teaching their baby to walk. When he falls down, they help him up and encourage him to keep trying. This can continue for months. No baby walks on its first try, but almost every baby does end up walking. For some reason, when people get older they get fewer tries to get something right. A baby will fall down hundreds of times before it learns to walk and will continue to fall from time to time, but it never gives up walking.

Often adults give up after one failed attempt. Some even give up before they make the attempt. The difference is the parents and the baby think walking is essential, while many adults do not consider their endeavors to be essential. When you look at finishing a project as essential, you will keep trying until you are successful. If you keep going until you complete the task, you will never be a failure.

Today get up and try again.

September 14

"Where there is great love, there are always miracles."
~ Willa Cather

The Bible tells us that God is love and that miracles come from God, so it stands to reason that where there is love there will be miracles.

Learn to love everyone and everything. Respect everything. When you start to live like this, miracles will start to show up in your life, and you will be more aware of the miracles all around you. There are miracles in your life right now. You just may not notice them.

When you give love to a person or a situation, that love will replace fear. Fear is darkness and love is light. When the light of love is shining on a situation, the fear is gone. When you can see the world in a new way, when you can see the world without fear, that is a miracle, and the more you do that, the more miracles you will notice in your life.

Today give love and expect miracles.

September 15

"Never do a wrong thing to make a friend or to keep one."
~ Robert E. Lee

Your life is yours to live, and through the years many people will pass through your life. If a friendship with one of these people exists because you did a wrong thing, then ask yourself, "Am I being true to myself?"

Be honest with yourself and those close to you. Share your principles and ideals if appropriate, but don't compromise your values. True friends will understand and respect you for standing up for what you believe. If someone does not respect your values, then he was not a true friend.

You are the only person you must spend the rest of your life with. Be true to yourself.

Today be a good friend but never lose yourself for anyone.

September 16

"If there be any truer measure of a man than by what he does, it must be by what he gives."~ Bishop Robert South

It is often been said that if you want more of something give it away. If you want more love in your life, then give love to everyone you meet. If you want more time, be willing to donate your time. If you want more money, tithe.

When you give of your time, your money, or your talent, what you've given will return to you. The world is a mirror.

It reflects back to you what you are. When you are giving, you live in a giving world.

Today give.

September 17

"No thing or person has the power to make you happy or unhappy. Your happiness is a result of your choice."
~ Unknown

You have the power to choose your mood. You can keep that power or give it away.

People give their power away by blaming other people or events. If you blame other people or events for your mood, then those people or events must change for you to be happy. Take 100% responsibility for your life. Only then do you have the power to change, the power to choose to be happy.

Today remember your happiness is your choice.

September 18

"A grudge is like being stung to death by one bee."
~ William Walton

When something happens that hurts your feelings or causes you to be angry or upset, it is not the event but rather your reaction to it that causes you pain. You could experience the same event without those negative reactions. Then you wouldn't feel the pain.

When you continue to hold a grudge, you are continuing the pain. The longer you stay upset, the more you are letting that single event hurt you. Your anger does not hurt the person you are mad at. It only hurts you.

Release your grudges, forgive yourself, and forgive everyone else. When you forgive and let go, you are open to receive love.

Today let go of your grudges.

September 19

"Happiness cannot come from without. It must come from within. It is not what we see and touch or that which others do for us which makes us happy; it is that which we think and feel and do, first for the other fellow and then for ourselves."
~ Helen Keller

Stop searching for the thing or the person that will make you happy. The only person who can make you happy is you.

Things and people can give you pleasure, but it is never lasting, and when it fades, you will start searching for the next thing to give you pleasure.

Help someone else. Give something away. Just sit in a chair and relax. Stop looking for happiness. Just allow happiness to flow from you.

Today let go and allow your happiness to come out.

September 20

"Most people are not going after what they want. Even some of the most serious goal seekers and goal setters are going after what they think they can get."~ Bob Proctor

If you are going to set goals and have dreams, make them big dreams. If you set huge goals and you miss, you get big results. If you set big goals and miss, you get average results. If you set average goals and miss, you get nothing. Stop being safe. Dare something worthy.

Today set one huge goal. Then work every day to make that goal a reality.

September 21

"Happiness cannot be traveled to, owned, earned, worn, or consumed. Happiness is the spiritual experience of living every minute with love, grace, and gratitude."~ Denis Waitley

Stop trying to find happiness. Happiness isn't something you find. It is something you are, something you experience. When you give love and learn to be grateful, grace will shine upon you, and you will experience happiness. You can be happy in any moment by giving love and being grateful. When you do this, you are choosing to be happy.

You can choose to be happy at any time and under any circumstances. Not giddy, but happy and at peace.

Today be happy.

September 22

"A man who is not afraid is not aggressive. A man who has no sense of fear of any kind is really a free, peaceful man."
~ Jiddu Krishnamurti

Aggression is just a way that fear projects itself. By being aggressive, we strive to prevent the thing we are afraid of from happening.

Many of us live from fear. Do you work because you love your job or because you are afraid of being homeless? When you love what you do and know that you are good at it, you have no fear of losing your job because you know you can find another job at any time.

One of the biggest fears is the fear of the unknown. Many people are afraid of change although they want their lives to be different. This is not a pleasant place to be - stuck in a situation that you don't like but afraid to do something different because it may be worse. The only way out is to face your fears.

List your fears. Write them on a piece of paper. Then pick one of the things on the list and do it. Make it something little. If you are afraid of snakes, go to a pet store and just watch the snakes for a while. Then maybe ask some questions about them. If possible, work up to the point where you can hold a little snake. As you cross your fears off your list, you will be more at peace.

Today face one of your fears.

September 23

"The art of living lies less in eliminating our troubles than in growing with them."~ Bernard M. Baruch

Our greatest trouble often reveals our greatest opportunity, but often we miss it. When we experience troubles or setbacks, we are often focused on the hardship and miss the blessing.

After a layoff, instead of taking the time to explore new and different opportunities, we sit and complain that getting laid off wasn't fair. We focus on how wrong it was rather than seeing the new adventure that has just shown up. Stop looking at the problem and find the benefit.

The difference between successful people and unsuccessful people is that successful people are constantly looking for the next opportunity and learning from their last problem.

Today if a problem arises, use it to see how you can grow.

September 24

"Nothing will ever be attempted if all possible objections must first be overcome."~ Samuel Johnson

There is a fine line between careful and immobilized due to fear. Careful can be good. I would never recommend being careless. However, the difference between people who are successful and people who just get by is that successful people take risks, calculated risks, but risks.

When opportunities arise, if you wait for all of the possible objections to be met, you will never get started. Get moving now and deal with any issues as they come up. Spending some time examining the opportunity first is always a good idea, but don't examine it to the point that you never start acting on it. Get moving. When you do this, there will be times when you do not succeed, but that's fine because there will be other times when you do succeed. If you wait for all the conditions to be safe, you will never do anything, and you can't finish if you never start.

Today just get out there and get moving.

September 25

"Humankind has not woven the web of life. We are but one thread within it. Whatever we do to the web, we do to ourselves. All things are bound together. All things connect."
~ Chief Seattle

This is a great way to look at the world. Whatever we do to the world affects us. The effect may not be noticed immediately, but it is there. When you say a kind and loving word to a stranger, you may brighten his day, so he in turn can brighten the days of others. When you accept someone without prejudice or judgement, you may show someone else that it is okay to live without hate. When you forgive, you may open up a flood of gratitude that affects hundreds or thousands of people.

How are you affecting the world and the people around you? Are you helping them or hurting them?

Today look at your impact on the world.

September 26
"What you are aware of you are in control of, what you are not aware of is in control of you"~ Anthony deMello

Awareness. Awareness. Awareness. Watch yourself. Can you step back and watch yourself? Can you observe your thoughts and actions? Can "I" see what "I" is doing? The "I" is who you really are. You are more than your body, more than your mind. When you can watch your mind and body in action, you will be able to turn your reactions into actions. You will be able to observe yourself moving through the world. Then you will be able to be in the world but not of the world.

Today be aware of the "I" inside of you.

September 27
"Don't ask what the world needs. Ask what makes you come alive, and go do it. Because what the world needs is people who have come alive."~ Howard Thurman

In other words, "Build it and they will come."

Do what you love! That desire was put inside you for a reason. Stop questioning it and go live it. Let go of the worries you have, and just move in the direction of your dreams. This can be scary at first, but you will succeed as long as you have passion and drive and are willing to work through your setbacks.

Today focus on what you want and how to make it happen.

September 28

"The components of anxiety, stress, fear, and anger do not exist independently of you in the world. They simply do not exist in the physical world, even though we talk about them as if they do."~ Wayne Dyer

Events are not good or bad, stressful or enjoyable, or happy or sad until you label them as such. Yes, acts of love and kindness are of a higher energy than acts of cruelty, but who determines what is kind and what is cruel? You do. You look at the circumstances and decide if something is good or bad.

If a man gives a boy $100, this would be considered kind. But if the man is his father and the boy has a twin brother who received $100,000 from his father, then giving the $100 could be seen as cruel. The difference is how you perceive the circumstances. The difference is you.

The only reason there is stress, fear, or anxiety in your life is because you say so. You get to choose how you react to events. You get to choose how you will live your life. When you choose fear, stress, and anxiety, the person you hurt most is you. Choose to eliminate these feelings by choosing to see the world in a different way.

Today choose to be happy.

September 29
"The secret of life is enjoying the passage of time."
~ James Taylor

The great Truths are always simple, and what could be simpler than this one? Life is made up of time, so if you want to enjoy life, enjoy how you spend your time. If you want to enjoy a bowl of ice cream, enjoy every bite. Don't focus on the destination, just enjoy the ride.

People get confused because the things they enjoy may be different than what other people enjoy. Stop worrying if someone else is enjoying himself and just enjoy yourself. When you stop concerning yourself with how other people live their lives, you will be much happier. Your happiness is not dependent on someone else being happy. You can be happy right now no matter what everyone else feels. Just enjoy this moment.

Today enjoy the passage of time.

September 30
Finally, what I really want is to be happy in this moment, where the magic and miracles happen. Stay in the moment and all gifts are added as you breathe and take inspired action."~ Joe Vitale

This is the only moment there is. Everything we ever experience happens now. Now is where all of your power is. The past is gone and the future isn't here. Anything you do, you do now. So decide to be happy now, in this moment. Release all of your fears and expectations and live in this moment. When you let go, inspiration will come to you and guide you. Moment by moment you will know what to do through inspiration. Few people are able to live like this all of the time, but if you can experience this just once in a while, it is great.

Today let go and live in the moment.

October 1

"All I want to do is learn to think like God. All the rest is just details."~ Albert Einstein

When you try to view the world from the point of view of God, things do change.

First is time, if time even exists for God. Your lifetime is just a blip in eternity. If you made a graph one mile long that represented the five billion years from the Big Bang until now, humans would only exist in the last two and a half inches of that mile, and an individual lifetime would only be the width of a human hair. When you look at things from that perspective, it makes the problems you have in your life seem almost insignificant.

Second is space. If the space in our galaxy were evenly divided between everyone on Earth, your nearest neighbor would be 400 light years away. And if the entire universe were equally divided between everyone on Earth, every person would get about 100 galaxies. In other words, the universe is so large that the human brain has trouble comprehending it. It is like asking an ant how big the solar system is. So when you think of the incredible vastness of the universe, the world as God sees it, our planet is very tiny.

Third is knowledge. You probably don't remember what you had for dinner last Tuesday, but God is all knowing and remembers everything that has happened every second of every day everywhere in the universe.

Our minds are not capable of thinking like God, but we can try to view life from a larger perspective. We can see the insignificance of the problems we are having. And then we can do what God does. Love everything and everyone.

Today try to see things from a larger perspective and practice loving.

October 2

"The theme that runs through my movies is the fact that we create barriers for ourselves....because we say, 'Well, I can't do that.' But in the end, you can't do it unless you can imagine yourself succeeding at it."~ George Lucas

You have to believe you can get where you want to go. Some people have great faith. They can visualize the end of a situation or problem and turn the details over to God, while other people need as many details as possible to keep their belief level high. Either way unless you can see the outcome, it is hard to start the journey.

Imagine the greatest vision possible for your life. Imagine it with all the detail you can. What would you do? Where would you go? Who would you talk to? Imagine with all of your senses - sight, sound, smell, touch, and even taste. Imagining is the first step to a new reality. Believing you can have what you imagined is the second. And taking inspired action is the third and final step. Don't forget about action. Once you believe you can do it, you need to go do it.

Today see it, believe it, and then make it happen.

October 3

"The pursuit of happiness is a most ridiculous phrase. If you pursue happiness, you'll never find it."~ C. P. Snow

There is no need to pursue happiness because you are currently happy. I realize you may not feel happy all the time, but happiness is inside you. You just need to remove the thoughts that are keeping you from experiencing your happiness. Then adopt new thoughts of happiness.

The first thought to think is that you can choose your mood. You can choose to be happy. After you make that decision, nothing can keep you from being happy except changing your decision.

Today allow your true happiness to come out.

October 4

"Nothing gives one person so much an advantage over another as to remain always cool and unruffled under all circumstances."~ Thomas Jefferson

When you can remain cool under pressure, you are able to think more clearly. When thoughts of anger or revenge come into your mind, you lose the ability to evaluate a situation.

Try to stay cool by looking at the situation from the outside. Pretend you are not personally involved and see if that changes your reaction. Allow yourself a little time to think about your response before reacting. When you are able to remain calm, you will be in a much better position to handle any situation.

When people realize they can't ruffle your feathers or control your mood, they will stop trying to. There are some people who either consciously or subconsciously enjoy controlling other people. They often do things in an attempt to make the people around them mad or upset. When you show that this no longer works on you, they will find another target.

Today be cool, stay calm, and remember happiness is a choice. Will you choose your mood or let other people choose it for you?

October 5
"Regret for wasted time is more wasted time."
~ Mason Cooley

We have all wasted time, and in the future we will waste time again. Facebook, reality TV, and video games are just some of the time wasters, but so is fear, worry and regret. It is a great idea to minimize the time you waste, but stop regretting it because that just wastes more time.

Move on and focus on what you are doing right here, right now. There are lots of methods to organize your life. Use one if you wish, but stop worrying about what you did or didn't do in the past. Focus on what you are doing now. Ask yourself, is this the best use of my time right now? It could be that you just need to relax or catch up with friends. Or it could be that you need to close your Facebook page and get to your to-do list. Whatever it is that will best serve your needs, do that.

Today ask yourself, what is the best use of my time right now?

October 6

"When you realize that there is nothing lacking, the whole world belongs to you."~ Lao Tzu

Look at nature. Nature produces everything in abundance. And the abundance of nature is effortless. People have been taught to believe in lack. Because of this belief, there is lack, but there doesn't have to be. When you believe in lack, you see lack. When you believe that lack does not exist, then you are open to the abundance of the universe. The world is then at your fingertips. Everything you could ever need or want is available to you.

See the abundance in your world, and when you have thoughts of lack, replace them with thoughts of abundance. Even if you don't accept the abundance at first, as you keep eliminating the thoughts of lack, abundance will become a part of your life.

Today focus on abundance in every aspect of your life.

October 7

"Do all things with love."~ Og Mandino

You can do this, and if you do, it will change your life.

The process is simple to explain, but you may need to work at it for a while to keep getting better. Before you take any action, ask yourself, why am I doing this? If the answer is loving and positive, then keep going. If your reason is not loving, then try to look at the action from a different view. Try to rethink the action so that it comes from loving energy.

For example, if you are about to pay your electric bill, you can think, I am paying this so that the power company does not shut off my lights. Or you can think, I am grateful for the luxury of having electricity in my home, and I am honoring my agreement to pay for this service I enjoy. Do you see the difference? The action is the same, but the energy is different. In the first example you are coming from fear, and in the second from gratitude.

If there is an action that you cannot instill with love, then it is a good idea to consider if you should take that action at all.

When you come from love in all things, your life will change.

Today think about your actions. Are you coming from love?

October 8

"If you judge people, you have no time to love them."
~ Mother Teresa

Often we get caught up in who is right and who is wrong, yet this does not serve us. Yes, there are times when you need the correct facts before making a decision, but the right and wrong I am speaking of has no direct effect on you. Imagine you are walking through the grocery store and you hear a toddler screaming at his parent. Do you assume something about that parent? The child? How the parent handles the situation? Does it meet your approval?

Next time this happens just send them love. Their life is theirs to live. You don't know their situation, so refrain from judgement and just smile. Wish them the best and let them live their lives.

When you allow the actions of someone else to affect you, you give up the power to control your life. When you are free of judgement, you can be happy at any time.

Today catch yourself when you judge, and change your judgement to love.

October 9

"When you're nice to people, they want to be nice back to you."~ Jack Canfield

What a great way to live, and it is even simple enough to teach your children. Anyone who has worked retail for more than a couple of months has had the experience of answering the phone at work and getting yelled at. He didn't do anything. He just answered the phone, and the person on the other end of the line is mad. For many of us our first reaction would be to get mad back, but this only increases the problem. By being nice to the person, he or she will start to calm down and the situation will improve.

Some people think the only way to get attention is to get mad. This isn't true. When you go through life being nice to everyone, people will want to spend time with you. Be the bright spot in someone's day. Be nice to people who don't usually get treated well.

Today just be nice.

October 10

"Whenever your feeling is in conflict with your wish, feeling will be the victor."~ Neville Goddard

Have you ever seen a new car that you wanted, but then felt you didn't deserve it or couldn't afford it?

Have you tried to use the law of attraction but got no results?

Have you ever wanted a romantic relationship to work but thought you were unworthy?

There are many times when you want something in your head, but your feelings are sending you a different message. When this is the case, you will never see your wish fulfilled. Your emotions are more powerful than your thoughts. Your emotions are running your life, usually without your knowing it.

Have you ever noticed when your day starts off badly, it usually gets worse? Or when your day starts off really well, it usually stays that way? Your emotions are controlling your destiny. When you feel great, you are more open to other situations that will allow you to feel great.

The best thing you can do for yourself is feel good. Make an effort to notice the good in your life. Be grateful. And when you feel bad, do what you can to change that feeling as quickly as possible.

Today feel good.

October 11
"There are no justified resentments."~ Wayne Dyer

I imagine right now you are trying to decide if you think that statement is true, and you are expecting me to try to convince you that it is. Instead, let's imagine how your life would be if you lived by that principle.

Without resentments, there would be no reason to get mad. When you resent someone, you are saying, "I don't approve of what you did." But did that person ask for your approval?

When you resent someone, it isn't about what that person did, it is about how you reacted to what he did, and if what he did caused you to feel resentment, you are giving control of your emotions to him. When you give someone else control over how you feel, then you are literally "out of control." You are letting someone else decide if you will be happy or mad, and that is just not a good way to live your life.

When you stop giving away control of how you feel, you can decide to feel good all the time. You cannot feel resentment and happiness at the same time, no matter how justified you feel the resentment is.

Today decide that *you* will choose how you want to feel. Don't give that choice away.

October 12

"The root of sorrow is attachment."~ Anthony deMello

Think about the last time you were sad. Likely it was because you lost something you were attached to or someone acted in a way you didn't like. In either case the thing you were attached to changed and it caused you grief.

The question this usually brings up is does this mean I can't love anything? No. It actually means you can love something for the first time.

When your love for your children is not dependent on what they do, then your children are free to be themselves. When you are telling your children, "I will love you if you get all A's," you are using your love as a negotiating tool. When you can love enough to let them be who they want to be, that is true love. You can give them advice and teach them. There can even be consequences for some of their actions. Just make sure they know you love them no matter what.

Love your friends by allowing them to be themselves. If they do something you don't like, tell them, but remove your expectations, your attachment to their actions. When you can do that, you will be happy no matter what they do.

Today let go of your attachment to something. Get to the place where you are okay with that item either being in your life or not being in your life. Then see how freeing that feeling is.

October 13

"A pessimist sees the difficulty in every opportunity; an optimist sees the opportunity in every difficulty."
~ Winston Churchill

There is an opportunity in every difficulty. Sometimes it's easy to spot, and sometimes it's hard to spot. The key to finding the opportunity is looking for it. Know that it's there and look for it.

When you get a new car, you start to see cars like yours everywhere. They were there before, but you weren't looking for them. You weren't aware of them. Now that they are in your awareness, you see them all the time.

The same is true with opportunity. Focus on the good, focus on the blessing, and that is what you will see. You can start to see opportunities all around you, and when you decide to act on those opportunities, your life will change for the better.

Today look for the good.

October 14

"Everyone is God speaking. Why not be polite and listen?"
~ Hafiz

Would you act differently if you knew everyone you met was God? How would you treat God if he came into your office? Well, I want you know God is a part of all of us. So everyone you meet is God, and everyone has things to say, so listen. Listen to what people have to say without judgement.

When you pray for guidance, be aware that your guidance can come from anywhere and anyone. It may come from a song on the radio, a commercial on TV, the book you are reading, or someone you see every day. Be looking for the message, and I am sure it will find you.

Today be aware and listen without judging.

October 15

"Acceptance of what has happened is the first step to overcoming the consequences of any misfortune."
~ William James

The past is the past. You can't change it. Whatever misfortune you have had, whatever wrong you think has been done to you, let it go. Accept that it happened and move on. So what if your last relationship ended. Move on. Who cares if you think you were cheated. Get over it.

When you spend time being angry about the past, you are only hurting yourself. You are the one who is carrying the baggage. You are the one who is continuing to suffer for what happened. Let it go. Accept that it happened, learn from the event, and move on. If the event hurt you in some way, stop the hurt and move on. The longer you hold on to the past, the more it will keep hurting you. Accept the past and be grateful for it.

Today accept the past and move on.

October 16

"Thousands of candles can be lighted from a single candle, and the life of the candle will not be shortened. Happiness never decreases by being shared."~ Buddha

Many people believe that if they give something away then they will have less of it. Just like elementary school word problems, if Johnny has five apples and gives three apples to Susie, how many apples does he have left?

If, however, Johnny has an idea and gives the idea to Susie, then they both have the idea, and they both benefit.

If Johnny decides to give love and happiness to Susie, then not only does Susie have more love and happiness, but Johnny's love and happiness increase too. And if they both continue to share this love and happiness, it can ripple throughout the entire world.

Emotion is energy in motion. As you give away love and happiness, their energy flows and increases, and both you and the receiver will experience more than you ever imagined.

Today give love and happiness to everyone you meet.

October 17

"Peace is not just a dream but a vibrant reality that exists within each one of us."~ James Twyman

You do have peace inside you. We all do. It is our nature to be at peace. When you are not at peace, it is because something is blocking your peace from coming out. Open yourself up to peace and let it flow from you.

When things happen in your life, ask yourself what is the peaceful thing to do? I don't mean let yourself be taken advantage of, just be nice. Being nice is very underrated. When you are nice, people want to be nice back to you.

Today be nice and let the peace and love within you come out. Remember that your peace must come from you.

October 18

"A warm smile is the universal language of kindness."
~ William Arthur Ward

When someone smiles at you it makes you feel good, and you smile back. And you know the difference between a fake smile and a real smile. We all do. Real smiles have an energy with them, an energy that cannot be faked.

So smile at people. Even smile when no one is around. It will make you feel better, and it will make everyone who sees you feel better too.

Today smile a lot.

October 19

"Respond intelligently even to unintelligent treatment."
~ Lao Tzu

From time to time you may meet people who act in a way that you don't agree with. They may get mad or irate. They may say things that you know are not true, and they may try to pull you into an argument. Stay at your higher level. It isn't your job to change the minds of everyone on the planet. If someone wants to believe something that you disagree with, who cares? Let him believe whatever he wants.

Do you want to be right or happy?

When you choose to be right, conflicts will be common. When you choose to be happy, you are able to respond to people at your level. You are able to be the light in the room. When you choose to be happy, you will discover that you can be happy all of the time, and isn't that what you want? Don't you want to be happy?

Today respond from your true self. Let the love inside you come out. Experience your happiness.

October 20

"If everyone demanded peace instead of another television set, then there'd be peace."~ John Lennon

When everyone wants peace, there will be peace. The only reason there is war is because people want war. When you decide that peace is the only option, the world moves one step closer to peace, not just peace between nations, but peace with each other.

You must take the first step. You must decide on peace. Show the world that you want peace by living in peace. When you choose peace, you are showing the world that it is possible to choose peace.

Today give peace a chance.

October 21

"Out of clutter find simplicity. From discord find harmony. In the middle of a difficulty lies opportunity."
~ Albert Einstein

Simplicity, harmony, and opportunity are the ways of the world. Clutter, discord, and difficulty are just illusions. Let go of the illusions and find the truth. You can transform any situation by transforming your thoughts. Focus on the good, and the good will appear. You are moving through a world that may seem very chaotic, but it actually works with complete harmony.

Look for the harmony in your life. Find it and your life will sing.

Today look for what you want to see.

October 22

"When you focus on being a blessing, God makes sure that you are always blessed in abundance."~ Joel Osteen

Blessings are all around you. When you start to look for those blessings, you will see them more often. Then when you see them, you will be able act on your blessings and use them to enhance your life. When you are a blessing to others, then the blessings that come your way will be multiplied.

Live your life to help others, using the gifts you were given. The more people you can share those gifts with and the more blessings you can give, the greater your contribution to the world will be. We all have a Divine purpose, and when we are living on purpose, we are a blessing to everyone we meet. When you live as a blessing, you are blessed both financially and from the love and happiness you experience.

Today be a blessing to the world.

October 23

"If I am what I have and if I lose what I have who then am I?"
~ Erich Fromm

Since many people have survived bankruptcy, and all of us exist before we own anything, the answer to the above question is that we are not what we own. Thinking that we are what we own is a way of letting our possessions own us. When you change this thinking, you allow yourself to be free.

You are a spirit created in the image and likeness of God, and since God is love, then you must be love. Since you are love, then you can give love to everyone you meet.

Today go forth and express who you are.

October 24

"Expect your every need to be met. Expect the answer to every problem. Expect abundance on every level."
~ Eileen Caddy

You choose your expectations. When you expect lack, then you subconsciously look for lack. Your ego wants to be right. Your subconscious mind controls much of what you do, so give that part of your brain a job that will help you not hurt you.

Expect great things. Expect abundance. Expect solutions. Expect everything to work out better than you planned. Continue to live your life exactly as you are doing now, just focus on the good not the bad. Focus on what you want to see more of. Focus on the things that bring you joy.

Today expect greatness.

October 25

"Doing what you love is the cornerstone of having abundance in your life." ~ Wayne Dyer

I believe this for two reasons. First, I believe we all have a purpose, and when we are living our purpose, life flows better. You are happier and more abundant when you are doing what you were meant to do, and life will reward you for fulfilling your divine purpose.

Second, doing what you love is where your talent lies. If your talent is growing plants, you shouldn't be an accountant. Likewise, if your talent is with numbers, you shouldn't be a gardener. I am not saying one is better than the other, just that you are likely to be better at doing what you enjoy. If you enjoy gardening, there is a good chance that you grow plants well. If you rate your skills on a scale of 1 - 10 with 1 being low, having a natural ability of 5 plus hard work can get you to a 9, but a natural ability of 1 plus hard work may only get you to 4. If your ability is a 9 you will probably make more money in that profession than a person whose ability is a 4.

So when you do what you love, you will get paid more for doing it, and the universe will reward you because you are living your divine purpose.

Today do what you love.

October 26

"What is necessary to change a person is to change his awareness of himself."~ Abraham Maslow

Nothing has more effect on who you are and where you are in your life than your opinion of yourself. If you think you are grumpy, then you probably don't have many friends. If you think of yourself as poor, you are likely in debt. But if you think of yourself as rich and friendly, then that is probably the case.

Lotto winners are a great example of this in action. Many people win huge sums of money and then lose it quickly. When the money just shows up, they still have the mindset of being poor, and that mindset doesn't change. Because of this their habitual mind influences decisions for them to become what they think they are, broke.

The great part of this is that it works both ways. If you want to have a loving relationship, then start to think of yourself as loving. Start to act in ways that are loving, and soon you will find yourself surrounded by people who love you.

Today think of the grandest, greatest you that you can imagine, and start to believe that it is true.

October 27

"You don't belong to you. You belong to the Universe and you're here to serve."~ Buckminster Fuller

This brings us to the age old question, why are we here? Your answer will impact how you live your life. How you answer is up to you. Buckminster Fuller believed you are here to serve.

When you live your life with the attitude that you are here to serve, it will affect the decisions you make. You will be helpful, caring, and compassionate. This is a great way to be. When you live your life to help other people, you will find you get everything you need in return.

Today decide how you can help others.

October 28

"When you are grateful, fear disappears and abundance appears."~ Tony Robbins

Gratitude is one of the strongest emotions. When we say thank you to the world for what we have, it allows more to come to us. But can gratitude eliminate fear? I think it can in two ways.

First, fear comes mostly from the unknown. If you are getting chased by a bear, you don't know if the bear will catch you, you don't know if you will live, and you don't know what will happen after you die. The unknown produces the fear. When we are grateful, we are saying that everything is good, and when we know the future will be good, there is nothing to fear, including death.

Second, we cannot feel good and bad at the same time. Gratitude is a positive emotion and fear is a negative emotion. We are not able to feel a good emotion and a bad emotion at the same time, so when we are feeling grateful, it is impossible to feel bad.

Today be thankful for what you have and open to receive the good the universe has in store for you.

October 29

"Always be yourself, express yourself, have faith in yourself. Do not go out and look for a successful personality and duplicate it."~ Bruce Lee

Examining the lives of people who have traveled the path before us is great. It lets us know what is possible. Having a mentor who can help you along the way is also a wonderful idea. Just remember to be yourself. If you are a martial artist, look at the life of Bruce Lee and see what he was able to do. See how he was able to go from nowhere to great fame. Look at what he did and know that those accomplishments are possible for you as well. But don't try to become Bruce Lee.

Be yourself. Allow your personality to come through. Put your own twist on things. Do what you do in a way that makes you special and different. Elvis was an amazing performer, and today there are many Elvis impersonators, but none of them will ever achieve what Elvis was able to accomplish.

Elvis also influenced an entire generation of performers. Artists such as Bob Dylan, John Lennon, and Bruce Springsteen all took that influence and made it their own. That is why they became great. When you are looking at others, use their ideas and their ways only as a starting point, but remember to have faith in yourself so you can be who you truly are.

Today be yourself. Let who you are shine through.

October 30

"I always have a wonderful time, wherever I am, whomever I'm with."~ Elwood P. Dowd from the movie *Harvey*

Having a great time is a choice. When we are with people who are having fun, it is easy to have fun. The energy of the other people is infectious. Getting caught in that energy makes it easier to raise our own energy. The mistake that most people make is thinking the other people make them happy. This is not the case. You are happy because you chose to be happy. The energy of the other people just makes happiness the easy choice. The same can happen when people around you are mad or upset.

Now you have knowledge that most people don't have. You know you can change your mood by changing your thoughts. When you are around people who are expressing emotions that you don't want to experience, change your thoughts. Think of a joke, a sunset, puppies playing, your children laughing, any happy thought, and focus on that happy thought until your energy is lifted.

As you practice this it will become easier until it is second nature. Then the visualization will not be necessary.

Today stay happy. Keep your thoughts on happy things, and don't let anyone get you down.

October 31
"Do not dwell in the past, do not dream of the future, concentrate the mind on the present moment."~ Buddha

This moment is all there is. When you focus on the past, you are giving your power to a memory. Learn from the past and then let it go. When you keep resentment, you hurt yourself not the people you are mad at. Let go of the past and live in this moment. Experience every moment for what it is. Fall in love over and over again from moment to moment. See a sunset for the first time. Look at the world with fresh eyes. Let this moment be new and creative.

Don't dream of the future. The only way you can influence the future is by what you are thinking and doing right now. Change the actions you take now and you can make your future what you want.

When you are focused on this moment, fear and worry disappear. Fear and worry are indications that you are thinking about either the past or the future. If you have ever had a traumatic event in your life, you know this. If your car is out of control, there is no fear. The fear shows up after the car has stopped, when you think back to what just happened. During the trauma you are focused on the moment, so fear does not exist. Ask yourself, why am I afraid of something that has already happened?

Today focus on this moment.

November 1

Inner peace can be reached only when we practice forgiveness. Forgiveness is letting go of the past and is therefore the means for correcting our misperceptions."
~ Gerald Jampolsky

Inner peace is a wonderful thing. When you have inner peace, your entire world is in harmony. The first step to attaining inner peace is forgiveness. If you are unable to forgive, there will always be uneasiness and drama in your life.

Often when we get together with family, old issues come up. Rather than reliving those old issues or blaming your parents for this, or your sister for that, just let it go. Let go of the anger, the frustration, the guilt, and even the resentments. Send love and forgiveness to your family. Your family is in part responsible for the wonderful person you are now.

Stop living in the past. Whatever event from your childhood you're still upset about, just let it go. Let go and enjoy this moment. Enjoy this time with your family. You're a different person than you used to be, and so is everyone else. Allow them to be themselves, and stop judging them for what happened in the past.

When you can do this, you will lead a much happier life, and isn't that what you want?

Today let go of the past and forgive.

November 2

"Don't ask the world to change — you change first."
~ Anthony deMello

This sounds very spiritual, but it is also very practical. The list of things you can change is much smaller than you think. You can influence things, but the only thing you can change is you. Only you can change your mind. Only you can decide what you will do. When you convince someone to change something about himself, all you are really doing is getting him to make a choice that you prefer. You haven't changed him, you have convinced him to change himself.

When you give up the idea that the world needs to change to agree with your way of thinking, you also limit the ability of other people to change you. When you can accept everything as perfect, reward and punishment will have little or no influence on you.

Today look at something you see as imperfect and ask yourself, "How can I change my perception to see that as perfect?"

November 3

"Live in the now because there is no other option."
~ Mark Rose

Now is the only time that exists. The past is just a memory of events, and when those events happened it was now. The future is a dream, and when it comes it will be now. So the only thing you can possibly do is live in the now because everything happens now.

The question is how are you using your now moments? Do you spend time regretting the past and worrying about the future? Or are you using this moment to accomplish something?

Today live each moment to the fullest, learn from the past, plan for the future, but live in the now. Live each moment to its fullest.

November 4

"If you think your life is about doingness, you do not understand what you are about. Your soul doesn't care what you do for a living-and when your life is over, neither will you. Your soul cares only about what you're being while you are doing whatever you're doing."~ Neale Donald Walsch

We are human beings not human doings. Your soul, the part of you that is you, is love. Your soul just wants to be expressed. By giving love and helping others you are living in line with your soul, your true self.

There may come a time when this reality can exist without us doing anything, but since we are not there yet, the next best choice is to do what you love. If you do what you love, and you help other people, you are in a great place. If you are in a job you don't like, change your attitude. There is no need to change what you are doing, just change your attitude. Change how you do it.

Today help as many people as you can, be thankful for all that you have, and love yourself.

November 5

"Many things can make you rich, but only a few things can enrich you."~ Robert G. Allen

Today think about what gives you the most joy and the most fulfillment. You may find that the most rewarding things in life are giving and helping others. Whatever gives you the most joy, spend your time focused on that.

Many people chase money hoping to find enrichment. However, if you find true enrichment, you will be wealthy beyond measure. Attracting abundance into your life is a wonderful thing to do, but it isn't the only thing. Use your talents to help others, and you will be enriched more than you can imagine.

Today focus on enriching your life.

November 6

"Happiness is as a butterfly which, when pursued, is always beyond our grasp, but which if you will sit down quietly, may alight upon you."~ Nathaniel Hawthorne

Many people think happiness is a goal that can be attained. If I can just get this last thing I want, then I will be happy. Happiness isn't found in cars, boats, or big screen TVs. It also is not found in jewelry, big houses, or designer clothes. Happiness is inside you, and it wants to come out. When you stop chasing after happiness, you can decide to just be happy now. Then the happiness inside you will come out.

Today stop chasing happiness and just choose to be happy now.

November 7

"At the center of your being you have the answer; you know who you are and you know what you want."~ Lao Tzu

Many people live their lives confused. They lack direction, wandering in the desert of the world with no particular place to go. But the answer is inside you. You know what you want. You know where you want to be. Look inside yourself. It is there. The big question is, once you know where you want to be, are you willing to move in that direction?

When you know what you want, be willing to get what you want. Be willing to do what you want. You may experience fear, but you have to move past the fear to experience the bliss. God wouldn't give you a dream without a way to fulfill the dream. I do not mean the desire of your ego, but the dream that is who you are, the desire that is inside you that is your life's purpose. That is why you are here.

Today find the desire inside you and start to fulfill it.

November 8
"Watch your manner of speech if you wish to develop a peaceful state of mind. Start each day by affirming peaceful, contented, and happy attitudes and your days will tend to be pleasant and successful."~ Norman Vincent Peale

You tend to get what you focus on. Have you ever noticed that if something bad happens first thing in the morning, the day takes a bad turn? Or if something great happens, the rest of the day is great? Events, either good or bad, can influence your attitude, and your attitude will influence your day.

When you start off your day thinking positive thoughts and making affirmations for the way you want your day to go, you set yourself up for greatness. As you go through your day and you keep those positive thoughts and words in the front of your mind, you will likely get what you want. When you think about the good, you will see more of the good.

Today think positive thoughts and speak positive affirmations.

November 9

"Love is always bestowed as a gift - freely, willingly, and without expectation. We don't love to be loved; we love to love."~ Leo Buscaglia

If you are a parent, think about how you felt toward your newborn baby. It was unconditional love, real love, because all real love is unconditional. When you add conditions to your affection, you don't have love, you have a contract.

When you love someone regardless of what he or she does or how he or she acts, then you have truly expressed love. And the feeling you get from doing that is like no other feeling in the world. When you experience it, it warms *you* even more than the person who receives it.

Try to bestow real love on the people you are close to. Love them and accept them for who they are without expectations or conditions. You may think this is an easy way to get hurt, but when you accept someone for who he is and love him completely, you will respect his decisions. Now, if his actions interfere with your freedom or happiness, you can choose to love him but not have him in your life. You can love an addict and accept his decisions without supporting the addiction.

Today love someone.

November 10

In the practice of tolerance, one's enemy is the best teacher."
~ Dalai Lama

Tolerance is a wonderful trait. We could all be a little more understanding and a little less judgmental, and people we don't like offer a great opportunity to perfect this quality in ourselves.

Most of the time we tend to agree with the people we like. The people we don't like often look at the world differently than we do. Listen to what these people have to say and try to understand their reasoning. You still may not agree with them, but when you understand why they think or feel a certain way, it will be easier to accept them.

Today practice tolerance.

November 11

"The moment you have in your heart this extraordinary thing called love and feel the depth, the delight, the ecstasy of it, you will discover that for you the world is transformed."
~ Jiddu Krishnamurti

Please read that quote again. When you have love in your heart, the world is transformed. Love is the most powerful force in the world. Love is the only thing that can turn an enemy into a friend. Love can lift you above fear, anger, and despair.

Divine Love is inside you right now, just like it is inside everyone of us. It can never be increased or diminished. However, you can choose to experience it or not experience it. That choice can change your life. When you choose to experience Divine Love, the world becomes loving.

Today experience the transformation. Choose to experience Love.

November 12

"Limited expectations yield only limited results."
~ Susan Laurson Willig

Think big. Many times people think too small. They want to be safe. They are afraid to dream too big because they don't want to be disappointed. The problem with that is low expectations can only produce small results. If you want big results, you have to think big.

Dream big. Raise your expectations. Get rid of the "good enough" mentality. You are better than that. Be happy and thankful for what you have, but know that everything you ever dreamed of is on its way. Don't limit your good by having small goals.

Instead of dreaming of peace with your neighbor, dream of world peace. Forget about just being able to pay your bills. Dream of being a billionaire.

Today whatever you dream, just make it big.

November 13

"Be content with what you have; rejoice in the way things are. When you realize there is nothing lacking, the whole world belongs to you."~ Lao Tzu

You are complete right here and right now. Can you have more in the next moment? Sure. Do you want more in the next moment? I hope so. But right now you are complete. And if what you desire in the next moment does not arrive, then you are still complete.

Imagine a wedding. A wedding only needs a bride, a groom, a witness, and someone to marry them. The dress, the tux, all of the guests, the cake, the photographer , the meal, the dance, the DJ, and everything else add to the event but are not necessary. The event would still be complete without them. And two people can be in love without the wedding.

You are complete, but you can add so much more to your life. Let go of the idea of lack. Don't fight it. Just let it go. Know that you are complete, and more will be added to you.

Today just know that you are complete.

November 14

"Today the greatest single source of wealth is between your ears."~ Brian Tracy

I believe that everything comes from The Divine, including wealth. We have been given tools that allow us to open the channel of that wealth. The tools are our mind, our intuition, and our emotions, and they can be sparked into action through divine inspiration. Like any tool, these can be used to help us or to keep us from our goal. A shovel can be used to dig for gold or to dig a grave. The tools you possess are even more powerful. They can build an empire or destroy one.

Look and listen for the inspiration. Then use the tools you have to create your empire. Everything you do is either moving you closer to your goal to moving you away from it. Pay attention to what you are doing so you can continue to move toward your goals.

Today open yourself to inspiration. Then take action.

November 15

"One of the nice things about problems is that a good many of them do not exist except in our imaginations."
~ Steve Allen

When we think of problems, they are almost always in the future, and since the future is not definite, then the problems may or may not come to pass. By all means take action now to prevent a problem if you do believe it is likely to happen, but do not waste your time worrying about issues that will never come up.

Focus on now and what you can do right now. When you get now taken care of, the future will take care of itself.

Today focus on the now and don't waste your energy inventing problems that will never happen.

November 16

Let us not seek to fix the blame for the past. Let us accept our own responsibility for the future."~ John F. Kennedy

When you have a problem in your life, do you look for someone or something to blame, or do you look for a solution? Blame may make your ego feel better, but it does not solve the problem. You need to take responsibility for where you are headed.

Your life is a result of the choices you have made. Your success or failure is because of you. If you think some outside force caused your failure, then you will also think success is impossible unless that outside force lets you succeed. And that is playing the role of victim.

As the victim, nothing is your fault. The problem with being a victim is you cannot change your life because you see yourself as powerless and helpless, always at the mercy of outside influences. To change your life, you must take responsibility for your life.

Accept that you are the one who got you where you are now, and you are the one who can get you to where you want to be. Stop blaming. Take responsibility. Move forward.

Today know that your future is your responsibility.

November 17

"If you never condemned, you would never need to forgive."
~ Anthony deMello

Forgiveness is a wonderful thing. I try to forgive everyone and everything. As I learn to forgive more, the time between my viewing something as a wrong and forgiving that wrong gets shorter. As I move through the thoughts of getting upset, I realize that if I am going to forgive someone in the end, why am I wasting my time now being upset or angry?

When you can experience something, anything, without reacting to it, you will never be upset again, and you will never have to forgive anyone again. You will be eternally happy. You may spend the rest of your life trying to live this ideal, but the concept is really quite easy to grasp. If you don't condemn another, there's nothing to forgive. And when you give love to everyone you meet, you will never have to forgive yourself.

Today forgive, but move toward a life where forgiveness is not needed.

November 18

"Remember there's no such thing as a small act of kindness. Every act creates a ripple with no logical end."
~ Scott Adams

The kindness you give to others is multiplied. When you help someone feel good, then they in turn can help someone else feel good , and so forth and so on. The results could be incredible. Your act of kindness could change someone's life, or it could inspire someone else to change the lives of millions.

Small acts are what create great deeds. World peace will not be because of some great act, but by individuals like you deciding to live a loving life. You can be an instrument of world peace by sharing love and kindness in little bits and pieces. Then the ripples can fill the world until the wave of love and peace consumes us all.

Today be kind whenever you have the chance, and know that the chances are all around you.

November 19

"I try to learn from the past, but I plan for the future by focusing exclusively on the present. That's were the fun is."
~ Donald Trump

That's where everything is. Everything is here and now. Everything you ever experienced was here and now. You can only be here. The here may change, but when you get there, there is here. And the time is always now. It always has been and always will be.

Stop waiting for something better. Have fun now. Stop wishing you were somewhere else. Have fun here. Focus on right here and right now.

Today focus on the present.

November 20

"Happiness is a continuation of happenings which are not resisted."~ Deepak Chopra

I have said before that real happiness is uncaused. Unhappiness comes from things blocking your happiness. When you resist what is, you are blocking your happiness. Stress, worry, and fear all come from resisting what is. They all come from focusing on a different moment than now.

Stop trying to change what is. It is a waste of time and energy. You can take steps to change the way things will be in the future, but first you must accept the way things are now. After acceptance, you can take action, but action only happens now, in this moment.

Accept what is and then move on, and you will be happy. Resisting what has already happened is like trying to defuse a bomb after it blew up.

Today let go of resistance and be happy.

November 21

"Let us always meet each other with smile, for the smile is the beginning of love."~ Mother Teresa

Mother Teresa loved everyone she met. She knew we are all children of God. Most people forget this. Most people look at the world as us versus them, but there is no them. They are us. When you can see everyone as us, when you can see everyone as a Divine child of God and know that you are the same, then you will understand true Love. Until then you can start moving in that direction by giving lots of smiles.

Smile at everyone you see. Laugh with the people you know well. Love the people you are close to in the way that God loves you. As you do this, the awareness of the love in the world will go up, and as more people realize we live in a loving world, more people will express their love.

Today smile and start spreading your love.

November 22

"The easiest way to get something is to give it away."
~ Mark Rose

I know this sounds backwards, but it is true. If you want to be happy, help someone else realize his happiness. If you want to be loved, love someone. If you want to be rich, help others become wealthy. I have a wonderful, loving, understanding, patient, and beautiful wife, and I make every effort to be understanding, loving, and patient with her.

The teacher often learns more than the student. What are you teaching to the people in your life? Are you helping others to achieve the goals you desire?

What is it you want in your life? When you know, figure out a way to help other people get it, and you will realize you have found it too. If you value success more than any other quality, then the more you help people find their success, the more successful you will become.

243

Today give the thing you want the most.

November 23

"He is a wise man who does not grieve for the things which he has not, but rejoices for those which he has."~ Epictetus

When we learn to focus on the good in our lives, we get more good. When we focus on the lack, we get more lack. You are wealthier than 90% of the people in the world. Focus on that. Focus on all of the abundance in your life.

Be grateful for all that you have, and what you don't have will be less important.

Today be grateful.

November 24

"Loving what you have and being in a constant state of contentment is the key to getting what you want."
~ Wayne Dyer

People often live their lives constantly wanting more. They want more money, more time, more love, and more peace. The problem is that when you are focused on what you don't have, you are not able to enjoy what you do have. When you are thankful for what you have, you open yourself up to receive more.

Everyone wants to be happy, and many people think that having the object of their desire will make them happy, but this is not the case. When you want something and you get it, you will often find yourself wanting something new very soon. And your happiness is then replaced with more wanting. When you are content and happy with what you have, then your desire for something new is much less. When you think, I love my car, and it does everything I need it to do, you can also think that a new car would be nice. But you are not putting your happiness on hold until you get the new car.

When you are content with what you have, you can be happy now. When you are happy, you are open to see the world conspiring to do you good.

Today love what you have and be open and ready to receive more.

November 25

"Never forget: the secret of creating riches for oneself is to create them for others."~ Sir John Templeton

This is true for riches, love, happiness, peace, and everything else. I have spent the last four years focused on enriching the lives of others. My goal is to make the world a happier place, and as a result I am very happy. I live every day blessed.

Look at your life and see if there is an area that you would like to improve. If there is, then spend time teaching or helping other people to improve that area of their lives. It is often easier to see what is holding your friends back than to see what is holding you back. But by helping them, it will be revealed to you.

Today start to teach what you want to learn. Give help in the area that you need help in.

November 26
"Like hatred, jealousy is forbidden by the laws of life because it is essentially destructive."~ Alexis Carrel

Nothing good comes out of jealousy, ever. When you understand jealousy, it is easier to overcome it. You are only ever jealous of someone who has a quality you wish to have. Jealousy is passive aggressive arrogance. Both qualities are usually rooted in a lack of self esteem.

When you become jealous, it is a good time to look at the situation and ask what quality does that person have that you would like to have. Then you can work to improve your self in that area if you wish. But remember to gage your improvement against yourself not others.

When someone close to you becomes jealous, just laugh. The more attention you give the jealousy, the more it will grow, so don't defend, don't argue, and don't console. Just laugh and tell him how ridiculous jealousy is. Then give him positive reinforcement to boost his self esteem.

Today avoid jealousy.

November 27

"Not all who wander are lost."~ J. R. R. Tolkien

It's great to have goals and direction in life. The easiest way to make sure you get where you want is to decide where you want to go. With that in mind, there are times when it is good to look around.

Spend time wandering around now and then so you can be sure that your goal is really the best goal for you. Spend time at work and at play. Spend time moving and sitting still. Spend time focused and time letting your mind wander. Life is about harmony, yin and yang. After time spent wandering, you may find the focus and clarity that eluded you.

Remember this too when dealing with young adults. Give them the time and space they need to find their own path. Then give them help if they ask for it, or let them find their own way.

Today know that it is okay to wander.

November 28

"The life that goes out in love to all life is the life that is full, and rich, and continually expanding in beauty and in power."
~ Ralph Waldo Trine

Most people can be put into one of three groups - those who love life and enjoy all that it has to offer, those who hate life and fight it every step of the way, and those who just exist but never live. The first two are full of emotion and passion while the third lives a life of quiet desperation.

No matter where you are now, you can join the first group. Let go of your anger, fear, and resentment, and love life. Send love to everything in your life. Start to notice things to be thankful for, and be grateful for everything.

When you send love into the world, it will return to you. When you become passionate about having a great life, you will have a great life.

Today love life.

November 29

"We can never obtain peace in the outer world until we make peace with ourselves."~ Dalai Lama

You can't give what you don't have. If a friend asked you for a dollar and you said you didn't have any cash on you, your friend wouldn't keep asking for the dollar. He would know that since you weren't carrying any cash, you couldn't give him a dollar.

The same is true with peace. If you are not at peace, you can't give peace, and you will not find peace in the world. The peace you desire is within your grasp, but you need to look within yourself to find it. When you have decided to embrace your inner peace, your outer world will become more peaceful.

Allow your inner peace to come through. You can do this by letting go. Let go of your attachment to an object or an outcome and see how doing this brings peace to the situation. Your peace can also be disrupted by internal conflict. When you give up the idea of fighting with yourself, when you stop blaming and shaming yourself, you start to experience peace. Remember the only place for peace to start is inside you. Your peace must begin with you, and my peace must begin with me.

Today make peace with yourself.

November 30

"Time is the most valuable thing a man can spend."
~ Theophrastus

Theophrastus was a philosopher who lived 2,300 years ago, yet even he knew the value of time. Today in our busy world this is even more important. We are constantly being pulled in different directions and have little free time. The information that we are flooded with makes our time even more valuable.

Learn to make good use of your time. Spend time both relaxing and working. Spend time with friends and family and time alone. Avoid wasting time. You can always make more money, but when a second is gone, it is gone forever.

Today use your time wisely.

December 1

"If you are willing to do what's hard, life becomes easy."
~ T. Harv Eker

The thing that is hard for most people is change. We all do things that keep us from reaching our highest potential. It could be a habit, a belief, or a thought pattern. Maybe you watch too much TV when you could be reading. Maybe you don't manage your time well. Maybe you buy things you don't need with money you don't have. Maybe you believe you don't deserve to be happy and successful. Or maybe you think you're going to get a certain disease because it runs in your family.

Whatever it is, most people don't want to change because they are afraid of what may happen. For most, the fear of the unknown is greater than the possibility of things being better. When you become willing to make a change, be it a change of a habit, a belief, or a thought pattern, then the possibility of things getting better increases.

When you make changes and then get out of your own way, life will flow and become easier.

Today be willing to make the changes needed to make your life easier.

December 2

"To love someone is to strive to accept that person exactly the way he or she is, right here and right now."
~ Fred 'Mister' Rogers

We all have times when we act in ways that we know are not kind or loving. We get upset over little things or we say hurtful things to retaliate. We use guilt or shame to get our way, but we never expect our actions will cause people to stop loving us. So when we love someone, we must also accept that he may occasionally do unkind or unloving things, and we must accept these less desirable qualities as well as his kind, caring, and companionate ones. Real love is unconditional.

Focus on the good, but when the less desirable qualities show up, do not withdraw your love. You can stand your ground and let the person know that you will not spend time with him if he continues to act that way, but tell him you do love him and accept him. Acknowledge and accept how he is acting without fear or anger and do not judge him as right or wrong.

Today accept people exactly the way they are.

December 3

"The only way to have a friend is to be one."
~ Ralph Waldo Emerson

When you think about the qualities you wish your friends had, be sure those are the qualities you develop in yourself. Nurture your friendships and they will grow. Spend the time to be a good friend. Become a person you would like to be friends with, and build relationships that will last for the rest of your life.

True friendship is not dependent on the time you spend with someone or how far apart you live. I have friends who live far away, and we don't see each other or talk that often, but when we do talk, it is as if we were never apart.

Today call a friend.

December 4

"Hate is not conquered by hate. Hate is conquered by love. This is a law eternal."~ Buddha

If everyone lived by Buddha's wise words, the world would be a different place. There would be no war, no violence, and no crime. But I can't force everyone in the world to be loving because forcing someone to feel or act a certain way is not possible. If I want the world to be more loving, and I do, the only thing I can do to bring about that change is be more loving myself.

There are times when it is easy to be loving. When we are experiencing love from someone else, it is easy to return that love. It is far more difficult to return love when someone gives us hate, anger, or fear. But the only way to overcome those negative feelings is to give love to them.

When I can give love for hate, I know that love can spread. The love I give will multiply, and if I want everyone in the world to live in peace and harmony, then I must live in peace and harmony with everyone. World peace starts with me right here and right now. When I can respond to hate with love, the world is one step closer to peace. And you are welcome to join me on my journey.

Today and every day I love you.

December 5

"If you want to reach a state of bliss, then go beyond your ego and the internal dialogue. Make a decision to relinquish the need to control, the need to be approved, and the need to judge."~ Deepak Chopra

Living this takes some practice.

The need to control can be strong. Try to let things go. Allow others to do what they think is best. The results may surprise you.

The need for approval is also strong. If you can do what you want to do without worrying about other people's approval, you are on your way to bliss. Begin by thinking about the people whose opinions you value the least, and try not to value them at all. Sing while you walk through a parking lot. People might think you are nuts, but why do you care?

The need to judge simply reinforces our need to be right or to be better than other people. We all form opinions about other people, events, and actions. Sometimes these judgements can help us, but mostly they limit us. Try to live an entire day without judging anything or anyone, especially yourself.

Today take one step toward bliss. All great undertakings are started the same way, by taking the first step. Take the first step toward your bliss today by relinquishing your need to control, your need for approval, and your need to judge.

December 6

"Simply put, you believe that things or people make you unhappy, but this is not accurate. You make yourself unhappy."~ Wayne Dyer

This is hard to accept the first time you hear it, but it is true. The people and events in your life do not determine your mood. Your reaction to those people and events determines your mood. Your mood is a choice. You choose how you will react. You chose how you will feel.

People often react without thinking. Reactions can be habitual, and choices can be subconscious, but they don't have to be. You can choose how you feel and how you react.

Today think about how you feel and choose to feel good.

December 7

"Just be happy now."~ Joe Vitale

Simple to read, slightly more difficult to do. But you can do it. Let go of whatever is bothering you and just be happy now. The problem can wait. The drama isn't that important. Just let it go and decide to be happy in this moment. This is the only moment that matters. What you do in this moment will determine your future. Take control of your future by taking control of this moment, and just be happy now.

Today smile.

December 8

"People often say that motivation doesn't last. Well, neither does bathing. That's why we recommend it daily."
~ Zig Ziglar

Often people will read a book or go to a seminar and learn a lot of great information that can change their lives, but as the days and weeks go by, the ideas fade, and the people fall back into their old ways of thinking. Motivation takes commitment. The more you are able to immerse yourself in new ideas, the easier it is for those ideas to become a permanent part of your belief system. Stay motivated and continue on your spiritual path every day.

There may be days when you slip from your routine or forget to motivate yourself. When this happens, don't feel guilty, just move on and motivate yourself the next day. As you continue to move forward, you will build momentum and it will be easier.

Today do something that will help you along your path. Read a book, watch a video, or talk to friends who are on the same path. Do something that will keep you motivated.

December 9

"The average person doesn't think well because they went to school."~ Robert Kiyosaki

School doesn't teach people how to think. For the most part school teaches people how to follow rules, and revolutionary thinking breaks the rules. If it didn't, it wouldn't be revolutionary.

Start to train your brain to think creatively. Puzzles and mind games can help, but the best training is thinking about ideas. Come up with new ideas. Then expand the ideas. Discuss your new ideas with friends and allow the ideas to grow. You may never implement the ideas, but the exercise will train your brain to think differently. Do this whenever you can. As you practice thinking creatively, you will get better at working through issues, and this skill will be a great help in your life.

Today try to think differently.

December 10

"Whenever anyone has offended me, I try to raise my soul so high that the offense cannot reach it."~ Rene Descartes

Remember that when you are offended, it has nothing to do with the other person. If you are offended, it is solely because of your reaction to the other person Your reaction is the deciding factor.

When you learn to change your reaction, you are raising your soul. We all want to be happy, and this is one of the secrets to happiness. When you decide that the words and actions of others are not going to offend you, you can be happy all of the time. The more you do this, the easier it is to do.

Pay attention though because if one offense is particularly hard to get over, it may be because you believe it yourself. When you spend two hours a day at the gym and your body is in great shape, someone telling you he thinks you should loose weight probably won't bother you. However, if you had to buy new pants that are a size larger than your old pants, someone suggesting you should loose weight might be very offensive.

When you get upset at what other people say, examine your beliefs and decide if you need to make a change in your thoughts, beliefs, or actions. Then rise above the upset.

Today choose to be happy.

December 11

"You are not paid to work hard. In fact, you are not paid for effort at all. You are paid for results. It's not what you do; it's what you get done." ~ Larry Winget

Many people are trading hours for dollars. However, the clerk at the convenience store is paid to help the customers, not just be at the store. If he showed up to work and never accomplished anything, he wouldn't last long. This is obvious to sales professionals. Visiting ten clients to get one sale is more work than visiting one client to get one sale, but the results are the same.

If you want to be good at your job, or if you want your business to be successful, focus on the results you are producing. Spend your time accomplishing more positive results, and you may find you are able to work less and accomplish more.

Today focus on the results.

December 12

"Gratitude for the abundance you have received is the best insurance that the abundance will continue."~ Muhammad

Thank you, thank you, thank you, thank you. It feels good to say that, doesn't it? Thank you, thank you, thank you, thank you.

When you say thank you and really feel the feeling of gratitude, you are opening up your life to more to be grateful for.

Take time every day to feel gratitude. You can be grateful for everything you see. Take time to feel that feeling. Feel gratitude and let your life expand.

Today feel grateful for everything.

December 13

"God didn't make a mistake when He made you. You need to see yourself as God sees you."~ Joel Osteen

The Bible says that when God created man he looked at his creation and it was very good. So God looks at you as very good. How do you look at you? God is all powerful and all knowing. God is perfect. You were made in the likeness of perfection by perfection, so you are perfect. You are exactly who and what you were born to be.

Within you is also the potential to be even more in the next moment. When you see yourself as God sees you, you are able to use your potential to become even greater. Yes, you are perfect right now, but you also have inside you the potential for much, much more.

Today recognize the greatness that is inside you and allow it to come out.

December 14

"If more of us valued food and cheer and song above hoarded gold, it would be a merrier world."~ J. R. R. Tolkien

Isn't that what we want? A merrier world? Don't we just want to be happy? It's great to be wealthy and live an abundant life, but why do you want wealth? Is it so you can be happy? You can be happy right now. Happiness is a choice, and it is easier to choose happiness when you are showing your love for another.

Get together with friends and family and show them your love. Show them you care for them. Then eat drink and be merry. Go to lunch with a friend, have a dinner party, visit your parents or your kids. Just spend time with people you enjoy spending time with.

Today call a friend and make plans to get together.

December 15

"The problem is the average person isn't tuned into lifelong learning or going to seminars and so forth. If the information is not on television, and it's not in the movies they watch, and it's not in the few books that they buy, they don't get it."
~ Jack Canfield

Learning should not end when you get out of school. There is more information in the world than you can ever learn, so keep studying and get better at what you do.

On a higher level, the quest for spiritual enlightenment is also never ending. Jesus of Nazareth said, "Even the least among you can do all that I have done and more." None of us has attained the level of Jesus, but we can strive to be more understanding, more forgiving, and more loving. And the desire for lifelong learning can help you get there more easily.

There are books and CDs and videos on almost every subject, but there is also another source. Inspiration is available to you at any time. When you close your eyes and get quiet, you can feel your connection with God and you can tap into divine knowledge. Use this source daily, or whenever you feel the need, or whenever you are unsure of what to do.

Whatever your source of knowledge and inspiration is, use it. Tap into that wisdom so you can learn and grow.

Today learn something.

December 16

"The question is not really whether or not you go on, but rather how are you going to enjoy it?"~ Robert Charman

This is an important question, especially after a trauma. After any event, big or small, it is time to move on. You may think that an event such as losing a loved one, losing a job, or ending a relationship is the end of the world, but it isn't. Sure things will be different, but your life has not ended. You can decide that your life is over and do nothing, but even that is a decision, and you are still moving on. Don't spend your time trying to relive the past. The past is gone.

The time to move forward is now. Explore new worlds - new worlds in your thoughts and in your experiences. Let go of the past and decide to make the best of today. By making the best of today, you pave the way for a better tomorrow, and you just might find that you're enjoying yourself in the process.

Today start moving forward.

December 17

"Happiness is neither within us only, or without us; it is the union of ourselves with God."~ Blaise Pascal

I like this quote, but I think the last part needs clarification. We are each always united with God. There is no other option. God is omnipresent, so if God is everywhere, that means God is in union with you. Happiness comes from our awareness of this union.

When you know that God is with you, and you believe in God's power, then what problem could you have that is too big for God? Knowing that God is with you allows the stress from every problem to disappear. You can allow life to flow without resistance.

If you have a different name for God or the Divine, this still applies.

Today know that God is with you always, and enjoy the peace and happiness that comes with that knowing.

December 18

"I can forgive but I cannot forget is only another way of saying I will not forgive. Forgiveness ought to be like a cancelled note - torn in two and burned up, so that it never can be shown against one."~ Henry Ward Beecher

Learn to forgive completely. Then move on. If you forgive someone but continue to remind him of the incident, you have not forgiven him. You still resent his actions and maybe even him. Let it go. Let go of the resentment and live in the now.

When you hold on to resentment, you are only hurting yourself. The pain and the anger is experienced by you. When you let go and forgive, you free yourself. The person you are mad at may not even know you are mad, but the pain and anger will keep you from fully expressing yourself in your life. The hate will keep your love from flowing. Forgive and allow your love to flow.

Today forgive and free yourself.

December 19

"You must take personal responsibility. You cannot change the circumstances, the seasons, or the wind, but you can change yourself. That is something you have charge of."
~ Jim Rohn

You are responsible for where you are. Other people have gone through similar circumstances and had different results. Your life is the way it is because of you. When you get out of the victim mentality, then and only then can you change your life.

Your problems aren't your parents' fault, your boss's fault, your spouse's fault, or your kids' fault. Your life is the way it is because of you.

Today take responsibility for your life and your actions. Then go out and create the life you want.

December 20

"Small minds discuss other people, average minds discuss events, and excellent minds discuss ideas."~ Clint McGee

What are you discussing? What do you think about? What thoughts occupy your mind? What do you and your friends talk about?

Your mind can be taught to grow. When you get together with friends, discuss ideas more and gossip about other people less. Instead of discussing what the politicians are doing or who is dating whom in Hollywood, talk about ideas to make your lives better. Many of the ideas may never go anywhere, but one great idea could change your life.

Discussing ideas may be tough at first, but it gets easier with practice. And the more you share an idea, the greater it can become. The more people who know about an idea, the more the idea grows.

Today come up with one idea and share it.

December 21

"To be happy we must not be too concerned with others."
~ Albert Camus

Society and especially the media try to get us to focus on others. The tabloids, the newspapers, the nightly TV news, and reality TV are all taking your focus off of you and putting it on others. Then they encourage you to judge what other people are doing, usually in an effort to make you feel better about yourself. The thought is, if you see people doing something you don't approve of, you will see yourself as better than they are. However, self confidence and self worth come from the self, not from others.

When you release your judgement of others, you allow yourself to be happy. When you shift your focus to yourself and take responsibility for your actions, you are able to move your life in a different direction. Happiness, self confidence, and self worth are all inside you now. Just release the thoughts that are blocking them from coming out.

One more thing to release is other people's opinions of you. What people think of you is determined not only by how you act and what you say, but also by their history and attitude. You can say the same thing to two different people and get two different reactions. Since you have no control over another person's thoughts, be true to yourself and allow others to think what they want.

Today focus on your true self and allow everyone else to be who he wants to be.

December 22

"The wise man puts himself last and finds himself first."
~ Lao Tzu

I know this sounds counterintuitive, but it is true. When you slow down and enjoy the moment for what it is, you won't care if you are in the shortest checkout line. You'll let the other car merge over in front of you. You will be okay with letting someone else get the credit. But more importantly, you will experience less stress, you will feel better, and the happiness inside you will flow out.

Allow others to be first and you will see your life growing in ways you couldn't have imagined.

Today be second.

December 23

"Ask, and it shall be given you; seek, and you shall find; knock, and it shall be opened unto you. For every one that asketh receiveth; and he that seeketh findeth; and to him that knocketh it shall be opened."~ Jesus Christ

What are you asking for?

Do you know how to ask?

The answer to the first question is easy. Look at what you have. That is what you have been asking for. If you do not like what you have, then it is quite possible that you do not know how to ask. Asking is a simple process that takes some effort and concentration. Then you will need to recognize the gift when it comes.

Ask for one thing at a time with both thoughts and actions. If you want to loose weight, concentrate on being thin, your desired result, not how much you weigh now. So to ask you must focus on the outcome that you desire. Then you must act in accordance with your desired outcome. If you ask to be thin while eating a half gallon of Hagen-Das, your actions are in conflict with your stated desire.

There will be times when the path to your goal is not as obvious. In those times listen to the inner voice leading you in a certain direction. This direction may not look easy, but it will feel right. Follow that urging and do what it takes to reach your goal.

The second thing is to make sure you are not asking for opposite results. If you want to loose weight, you can't think of yourself as fat. You may know that your body is fat, but when you know that the true you is thin, your weight loss will be easier.

Today focus on the result you desire.

December 24
"What a child doesn't receive he can seldom later give."
~ P. D. James

This is obvious in the physical world. If you want to give a fruitcake, you must have a fruitcake. Well the same is true in the emotional world. If you want your child to give kindness, then you must give him kindness. If you want her to give love, than you must give her love.

People will give what they have been given. When you give your children anger and frustration, that is what they will give to others, and if you fail to give them emotional support, they will lack the empathy and compassion needed to deal with

267

their friends. People will always give to others what they have been given.

Today give love and kindness to every child you meet, whatever his age.

December 25
"It's not how much we give but how much love we put into giving."~ Mother Teresa

Have you ever given a gift that you were not sure the receiver would like? You looked and looked and couldn't find anything, so you just picked something and got a gift slip to go with it? We have all done this. The secret to great gifts is love. When you put love into the entire giving process, you will be led to the perfect gift.

Think lovingly about the person when shopping, buying, wrapping, and giving the gift. Send him love as he opens it, and even if he doesn't like the gift, he will still feel the love you put into it.

And if you give to a charity, send the check with love. Don't write the check until you can send love with the gift.

Today make every gift special by giving from the heart.

December 26
"Gratitude is the open door to abundance."~ Yogi Bhajan

Gratitude comes in two forms. You can be thankful for what you have, and this is wonderful. I am thankful every day for everything in my life. However, the second type of gratitude is more powerful.

When you can be thankful for the things you do not have, that is very powerful. I do not mean being thankful that you don't have the flu, but be thankful for the abundance that you know is coming your way. Be thankful for the perfect lover even though you have not met him or her yet. Be thankful for your next car.

When Jesus fed 5,000 people with five loaves and three fishes, he was thankful first, then the food appeared. Be thankful now and know that all that you desire is on its way to you.

Today be thankful for what you have and for what you wish to have.

December 27

"After you've done your best to deal with a situation, avoid speculating about the outcome. Forget it and go on to the next thing."~ Unknown

Do your best then move on. This is hard to do. We are often worried and wonder about how a situation will turn out. The thing to remember is after we do all that we can do, there is nothing more to do. If there is something more you can do, then do it.

When you are done, have faith that you did your best and enjoy the results. When you are thinking about what you have done, then you are not thinking about this moment and what you can be doing in this moment. This moment is what matters. Let go of the past and move onto the next task.

Today do your best. Then move on.

December 28

"Happiness is a way to take the journey. It's not the destination."~ Mark Rose

Many people live their lives thinking, "I'll be happy when I get that new car, or when I get that promotion, or when I meet that special someone." I am here to tell you that your happiness cannot come from outside of you. The car, the boat, the lover, the money--none of these things can make you happy. When you get one of these things, like that car, you may choose to be happy. But as long as you believe that car is the source of your happiness, disappointment is close at hand.

Happiness comes from within. As long as you believe that you need something, you will never be truly happy. Decide to enjoy the moment and be grateful for what you have now. The future has many great gifts for you, but happiness can only be enjoyed in the present. Happy people are ones who have chosen to be happy, and they live their lives expecting more good. Don't look for happiness in your possessions. They are not you and they are transient. You will find happiness in the only permanent part of your life, your spirit, or your soul, the always present part of you that is you. When you find your happiness inside of yourself, you will also realize that it can never be taken away from you.

Be thankful for all that you have and all that you are, and know that tomorrow can be even better. Don't wait for some event that may never come to be happy. Accept that your true state of being is happiness and accept it now.

Today choose to be happy and grateful for where you are and for all that you have.

December 29

"A ship collects more barnacles in the harbor than it does at sea."~ Zig Ziglar

Ships were made to sail, and people were made to live. When a ship sits in the harbor, it becomes less and less seaworthy. When a person lives in the past, he or she becomes less and less able to live in the moment.

Life is meant to be engaging. Do something. Experience something. Be something. But don't just turn your mind over to TV producers. Your life is yours to live how you wish, but you must live it, or you will waste it.

Today experience life.

December 30

"In the long run we shape our lives, and we shape ourselves. The process never ends until we die. And the choices we make are ultimately our own responsibility."
~ Eleanor Roosevelt

You are constantly creating your life. The events in your life do not create who you are, your reaction to those events creates who you are. You choose how you will react to life, and your choices produce results. If you are not happy with the results you have been getting, then you need to make different choices.

The question then becomes, what choices have I been making that do not serve me? And although I do not know your specific choices, I do know this. When you live your life from a place of love and gratitude, life will flow easier. Then find your divine purpose and spend a large part of your time fulfilling that purpose.

Today choose how you want your life to be, and make choices that will create the life you want.

December 31

"To love for the sake of being loved is human, but to love for the sake of loving is angelic."~ Alphonse de Lamartine

When most people think of love, it is not unconditional love. Love with a capital L is Divine Love. It is Love that has no beginning and no end and no conditions. It is just pure Love.

That pure Love is God, and when you see Love, it is God expressing.

Think about the people you love. Then ask yourself if they stopped doing the things you like, the things you want them to do, would you still love them? If you said yes, then you are giving them true Love. If you said no, that is okay, even typical.

If your spouse or a loved one doesn't behave the way you expect him to, do you withhold love or even withdraw it altogether? If so, try to get past this. When you decide to love someone with no thought of getting anything in return, the person you love is free to be who he truly is, and you are expressing who you truly are.

Love without expectations. Love for the experience of being Loving. With practice you can do this. It is your true nature. It is what you are. God is Love, and you came from God, so you too are Love.

Today and every day, express your Love.

I hope you enjoyed reading this book as much as I enjoyed writing it.

We are entering a new age and there are so many people who are waking up to the ideas that I share in this book.

As I continue to write and put on workshops, I want to know what you are interested in. What are the issues you are facing? I want to know what I can do to help you most.

Please visit my website www.AcceptHappinessNow.com. You can send me an email, sign up for my newsletter, and find me on social media.

I would also love to hear your thoughts on this book. I answer all of my own emails, so please feel free to send me a note.

Peace Begins with me,

Who is Mark Rose?

Mark Rose is a teacher with a mission. He has spent the last twenty years on a spiritual journey to find himself and the keys to happiness. After reading hundreds of books, studying thousands of people, and allowing inspiration to guide him, he has become happy and peaceful. Although his journey to enlightenment is far from over, he wants to share what he has learned with you, so that you too can experience true happiness.

Mark's message is simple. He wants to show you how to live a life filled with happiness, love, joy, peace, and abundance. Mark takes the wisdom of the ages and shares it in simple, easy to understand terms, while also giving you tools you can use in your everyday life. His messages are insightful, inspiring, uplifting, and at times even humorous. His passion for his beliefs is evident in his writings, and his commitment to sharing these beliefs with the world is commendable.

Mark lives with his wife, daughter, and two dogs in Kansas. He enjoys spending his free time with his family and friends, sailing, reading, and volunteering for the local animal shelter. You can learn more about Mark at

www.365Inspirations.net
www.AcceptHappinessNow.com
www.MarkDRose.com
www.HeavenOnEarthProject.com
www.NormalSucks.net

www.ingramcontent.com/pod-product-compliance
Lightning Source LLC
LaVergne TN
LVHW051458080426
835509LV00017B/1812